CULTIVATING
SPIRITUAL CONNECTION:

7 TOOLS TO GROW A LIFE OF
LOVE, JOY, PEACE, AND ABUNDANCE

Wendy E. Crane

www.solflowerwellness.com

Cultivating Spiritual Connection:
7 Tools to Grow a Life of Love, Joy, Peace, and Abundance
By: Wendy E. Crane

Wendy E. Crane, LMFT
Sol Flower Wellness
200 Waymont Court, Suite 126, #1
Lake Mary, FL 32746
(407) 739-4267
www.solflowerwellness.com

To Mom and Dad for helping me to see God in all things,

everywhere, and for nurturing and encouraging my own spiritual

connection through nature, love, and the deep understanding that

prayer is powerful, I always have choices, and I am never,

ever alone. I love you both.

Thank you from the bottom of my heart!

Table of Contents

Introduction 1

Preface 3

Chapter 1 : Discovering Connection 7

Chapter 2 : What Inhibits Your Connection? 17

Chapter 3 : Tools for Cultivating Your Path 37

Chapter 4 : Journaling—A Dialogue with the Divine 45

Chapter 5 : Prayer—Start the Conversation 55

Chapter 6 : Meditation—Listen for the Knowing 65

Chapter 7 : Yoga—Breathe In/Breathe Out 75

Chapter 8 : Music and Mantras—Calling in Spirit 85

Chapter 9 : Ritual and Ceremony—Anchor Your
Connection 93

Chapter 10 : Nature—Spirit Is Everywhere and In
Everything 115

Chapter 11 : Living the Promises of Love, Joy, Peace, and
Abundance 125

Chapter 12 : Go Forth and Cultivate! 131

Recommended Reading 133

Recommended Playlist for Chanting, Meditation, and
Inspiration 137

Acknowledgments 143

About the Author 145

Introduction

L ife only moves forward. You can move with it, or you can resist it, but the direction never changes. You can drift aimlessly through life, or you can plug into a Source of energy, guidance, cooperation, and love that is you and much larger than you at the same time. When plugged in, you will feel more supported, guided, and protected and more in tune with the flow of the Universe. You plug in by creating a spiritual connection with your interpretation of this Source energy.

Spiritual connection has been a lifeline for me through every chapter of my life on the planet thus far. It weaves through all aspects of my daily living. I love to discuss spiritual concepts and learn about how spirituality fits into the lives of those around me. My inspiration to write this book was to share what I have learned along the way, encourage you to discover your own connection, and support you in cultivating a relationship with something greater than you. This is not a religious book, although it will periodically reference aspects of different world religions and other spiritual concepts.

You are in charge of how you choose to visualize or conceptualize what you are connecting to. You might visualize a person or being, like Jesus or Buddha, or think of it as light, energy, or the Universe. It may be more of a feeling, like being embraced in a big hug or surrounded by support or comfort. Or you may sense it in your body as tingling, warmth, vibration, or weightlessness. You can pull from any religious tradition that may be in your upbringing or discover it through yoga, music, chanting, or the simple symbols of Spirit that surround us in our everyday lives in the trees, the wind, the clouds, the sun, and other expressions of nature's mystery. The choice is yours. It is available today, and this book is here to help inspire you and provide you with a companion for your journey.

Read these pages from cover to cover or randomly open a passage you feel drawn to in the moment. You may also find these messages useful as prompts for meditation and/or to inspire a journal entry. This book can accompany you during a trying or transformational time in your life or propel you into an expansion period of growth and learning. May you use it as a stepping stone to pave your path and to remember your connection when you forget. This is an offering from my heart, and I send it to you with love. Happy reading!

Preface

Thank you, Lord, for each new day you give to me:
For earth and sky and sand and sea,
For rainbows after springtime showers, autumn leaves,
and summer flowers,
Winter snowscapes so serene, harvest fields of gold and green,
Beauty shining all around, lilac scent and robin sound,
For stars that twinkle high above and all the people that I love. Amen.
~ Author Unknown

At five years old, words appealed to me. I liked the way they went together and the different sounds and rhythms they made. I loved nature and the outdoors. I was curious. I loved to pick wildflowers, watch birds and butterflies explore their world, examine the different colors and shapes of leaves, see animals in the wild, listen to the wind, look out at vast views, and smell earth, rain, snow, and fresh air. As I continued to grow, I cherished the seasons and how the air would change as the year went on. I was drawn to the colors and the smells and using all my senses. I loved God even before I knew what that was.

My mom and dad recognized this in me and helped me nurture it. One morning after church, there was a market of sorts selling wares for a church fundraiser. My father picked out a poster for me that had the above prayer printed, complete with colorful crayon-like illustrations of the various aspects of nature, and displayed in such a way that was quite appealing to my kindergarten understanding of life at the time. Who knew how profound these words would be and how they would sustain me well into midlife?

When my father presented this poster to me, I was enthralled with it. On my wall, it hung through every year of my life— through house moves, adolescence, college dorm rooms, and long after college. It wasn't even in a frame until I was thirty and pregnant with my son. Once framed, it hung above my son's crib and then over his bed while he grew up. However, the poster did not seem to make the same impression on him. He felt supported by the prayer, but when he got ready to leave home for college, he did not feel the same need to carry it with him as I did.

I eventually realized that he would not carry the physical form forward because it was meant for me, but the prayer lived in his heart. So, I reclaimed it again, and now, it has found a permanent home in my meditation room. It's one of the few prayers I have memorized and held dear within my heart. It is accessible anytime I need to say, "Thank you." It reminds me of the most important things and reminds me to be grateful.

When I look at this poster and this simple, precious prayer, I see the essence of my true self. The deepest, most sacred part of me can be summed up in these beautiful words and symbols, simple enough for a five-year-old girl to grasp and attach to and deep enough for a fifty-year-old woman to continue to connect with and expand around.

I thought it fitting to begin our exploration of how to cultivate spiritual connection with this message of gratitude, as it was part of my humble beginnings. Through the years, I've evolved, and my mantras, prayers, and ways of connecting with something larger than me have expanded, but the root of my entire spiritual experience is gratitude. For that, I am truly grateful.

The following chapters are intended to inspire you to find your own words and ways to connect with something bigger than you and recall when you first connected to your spiritual nature.

How old were you? Did someone share something with you? Were you inspired by something or someone? What teachings appealed to you? Where in nature do you connect most with spirit? Where do you feel safe? Explore these questions in your journal or in your next meditation and see what comes to you. What are you most grateful for?

My father wrote on the back of this poster twenty-five years after gifting it to me when we had finally put it into a frame. It is from his knowing and seeing me, along with my mother's support and encouragement to foster my relationship with God in all forms, that I can share this book with you today. In his own words:

> *Wendy (My Little Princess),*
>
> *I bought this poster for you twenty-five years ago when you were only five years old, and it was now time to finally frame it so it doesn't fade or deteriorate. It symbolizes everything you represented and meant to me back then and still do and always will. When I see*

butterflies, birds, rainbows, flowers, and all of God's beauty, I think of you. You always loved everything about nature and beauty that was provided to us each and every day. I know that you will always be thankful, as I will, that nature and beauty and love surround you constantly. You are part of the beauty in my life that I will be forever thankful for.

I love you with all of my heart and always will, and you will be my Little Princess forever. I love you, Dad. (May 4th, 2003)

Chapter 1

Discovering Connection

A re you tired of feeling anxious, overwhelmed, and alone in this world full of information, distractions, and a seemingly limited amount of time and resources? Do you often feel powerless or overwhelmed by all the pressures life seems to produce? Maybe you feel pulled in a million directions and have lost track of who you truly are or want to be, instead struggling to get through the day and respond to the incessant messages that flood your phone.

I always know when I am struggling with something by the number of books piled on my bedside table. Typically, I am searching for an answer, reassurance, a sense that I am somewhat normal, or the answer that will make life more manageable or help me feel at peace with life or myself. When I first entered perimenopause, I devoured six books and spent endless hours scrolling Google on the topic, seeking relief from the initial symptoms and confusion that accompanied them. Surely, someone had written something that would help me feel better! What sends you looking for answers? Where do you go searching? Have you ever found exactly what you were seeking? Neither have I.

Where I always end up is a teeny bit further down the road but mostly more confused, and ultimately, I am left with myself. All those books gave me some useful information but did not tell me about myself. I tried many tricks and solutions, but there did not seem to be one true path to make menopause enjoyable. (That may have been my first mistake! Certainly, my first step would need to be adjusting my expectations.)

But always, at some point, I reach a point of surrender and have an *on-my-knees* moment where I let go of needing to find the answer, and I check in with myself. Once I settle down enough to tune into the wisdom offered to me in silence, meditation, or in the quiet moments in nature with myself, I arrive at a point of clarity, and the next right step is revealed. It may not be a complete transformation in that moment, but it tends to point me on a trajectory that leads to greater acceptance and a deeper understanding of myself, and *this* helps me to feel more empowered and clearer about what I actually need. This process was here for me all along. But it is so easy to forget.

Because of all the external forces and unseen expectations from our families, friends, and culture that we face daily, it makes sense that we might first look outside of ourselves for a sense of relief from whatever ails us on the inside. Google, social media, and podcasts have replaced our inner GPS and encouraged us to forget that most of the answers to our dilemmas can be found by going within rather than seeking outside answers.

When you go within, you foster a connection with your deepest, most true, and highest Self. I refer to this as Self with a capital "S." This begins your relationship with Spirit or whatever you choose to call the greater energy surrounding you. This connection helps you to see a more expansive viewpoint and offers endless wisdom. It is with this energy that I am calling for you to cultivate a connection. For simplicity's sake, I refer to this as a *spiritual connection*.

You may already have a deep spiritual connection, and I hope the tools I share with you will help to deepen it further. Or they may help you remember something you have long forgotten or even help you reveal something new that you never considered available before. When everything else in life pulls you to look outside yourself, the experiences and strategies I share will help direct you inward to your spiritual source, where you have unlimited power, unlimited potential, and the capacity to make anything happen. A solid spiritual connection also helps relieve feelings of anxiety, isolation, and loneliness by redirecting you back to your most powerful resource: Spirit within. When you are connected to this powerful source, love, joy, peace, and abundance are readily available and have the potential to expand your life beyond anything you can imagine.

The nature of the spiritual connection is totally up to you. You are in charge of defining the relationship you develop and how you choose to visualize or conceptualize what you are connecting to. There are infinite ways to access it. Explore how journaling, prayer, yoga, music or chanting, meditation, ritual, and the simple symbols of spirit that surround us in our everyday lives—the trees, the wind, the clouds, the sun, and other expressions of nature's mystery—clarify your relationship to the Divine. Or you may draw inspiration from any religious tradition in your upbringing or that interests you. The choice is yours.

I have been a spiritual seeker all of my life. I come by this drive honestly. The roots lay in my late grandmother's three-word spiritual philosophy, "God is Love." Whenever anyone asked her about her faith, she would reply with those simple yet profound words. She was an artist who painted beautiful watercolors of flowers and other splendorous nature scenes. I witnessed her tending to her garden, helping me understand the wildflowers growing in her yard and learning which birds visited her birdbath. This statement that *God is Love* took me into midlife to fully grasp, and it continues to reveal deeper meaning as I evolve through life. My understanding is that if God is Love, then Love is God, and God is within the exchange of love and love itself. And if this is true, there is nothing else—no need to fear or get lost in the egoic nature of the human mind and all that it creates to distract us and attempt to complicate something so simple.

I grew up within a progressive Christian faith with permission to explore and expand and see that God is as Shug Avery so poetically expounded in Alice Walker's *The Color Purple*:

"Here's the thing, say Shug. The thing I believe. God is inside you and inside everybody else. You come into the world with God. But only them that search for it inside find it. It ain't something you can look at apart from anything else, including yourself. I believe God is everything, say Shug. Everything that ever was or ever will be. And when you can feel that, and be happy to feel that, you've found It."

My mother built upon my grandmother's philosophy with the addition of what I would now call "Spirit as Nature." She and my father helped me recognize God in the mountains, trees, ocean, lakes, and sky. John Denver was the soundtrack to my family's Saturday mornings and long car trips. By age ten, I had memorized all the words to most of John Denver's songs. He seemed to share a similar viewpoint, and his songs reinforced my family's teachings. I began to see Spirit all around me, through me, and in everything I encountered.

One song in particular has always stuck with me, titled "Windsong." It describes the wind as a force that is both mother and father, earth and sky, watching over you and gently nudging you to listen and to lean into the support. The wind is a messenger, a carrier of knowledge, and a deliverer of joys and warnings. The wind is all around you and moves through you. When you hear the song and take in the beautiful message, the wind becomes a source of divine energy. When I sing "Windsong," I feel that energy. The next time you feel the wind on your face, notice if you can sense the power within it.

Because of my Christian foundation, I tend to instinctually refer to this larger spirit as "God" but have also evolved into interchangeably calling it "Spirit," "The Universe," "All," "Benevolent Forces," "Life Force," "Energy," "Source," "Consciousness," "Love," "Presence," and whatever other word or name seems to fit something so immense and beyond my understanding that it really cannot be named or constrained to fit into a human construct. I will use most of these terms throughout this book. Know that, for me, they all refer to the same thing.

I do not believe there is more than one energy source in this universe. I believe it is all the same, no matter how it is expressed or conceptualized. I am aware that not everyone on this planet thinks this, but for the sake of this book, please know this is the perspective I am sharing. I also learned from Eckhart Tolle a long time ago, when he and Oprah were doing their video series on his book *A New Earth*, his perspective on God and adopted this understanding. Tolle purported that God, or whatever we choose to call this unmanifested presence, does not have an ego and, therefore, does not have a care or an expectation of what we call it. It is meant to be experienced and known rather than defined.

I spent my undergraduate years in Pennsylvania at Bucknell University studying counseling, women's studies, and religion. I became fascinated with the similarities that seemed to thread through many of the origin stories of these religious traditions and how the different spiritual master teachers appeared to share a core message that aligned with my grandmother's teaching. At the heart of every faith, underneath all the rules, dogma, rituals, etc., was love and a supportive force that seemed to hold space for all souls in the universe. This seemed to validate my grandmother's and parents' teachings and solidify my understanding as much as I could grasp in those years.

My women's studies and social justice curiosity drew me toward an inclusive view of our shared human experience. I struggled back then and continue to struggle with the division that exists over something that seems simply universal to me. But I also came to understand that as humans, we tend to complicate things in our attempts to attach to them and often feel a need to compare and separate things from each other. This has always deeply troubled me but continues to draw me toward seeking and understanding the nature of Spirit and how we can all connect to it and each other.

After I graduated college, I ventured off to Breckenridge, Colorado, to spend a year skiing and working in the mountains and to get clear about my next step into graduate school. I lived and worked in a bed and breakfast called the Fireside Inn, where I worked three days a week and made $30 a week, plus room and board. I earned just enough that first summer to afford a ski pass for the season. I endured some crazy roommates and lots of cleanup after messy boys who were the primary visitors to the youth hostel attached to the bed and breakfast. But my favorite days were when I did not work and could roam around town on my bike or hike into the mountains. And, of course, once the snow came, I skied to my heart's content.

Skiing was a huge part of my growing up. I learned to ski as a little girl and realized that if I was good at skiing, I could get to the top of the mountain and make my way down on any slope available. But the goal was not to be the best skier. It was to get to the top of the mountain because that is where God lived, as far as I was concerned. And I wanted to get as close to God as I could.

During that year in the Rockies on top of the world, I came to understand what John Denver was talking about in *Rocky Mountain High* when he refers to how simple and easy it is to access and speak to God from those peaks. I heard and felt the presence of something supportive, loving, patient, and all-encompassing in a way I did not understand before. I felt it, *knew* it, and wanted to feel as close to this energy as possible for the rest of my life.

I would exit the T-bar at the top of Peak 8, ski off to the side, remove my skis, and sit, taking in the view. I could feel the chilly air on my exposed face, breathe in the fresh smell of snow and pine trees, and take in the gorgeous blue sky, white mountains, and the tops of green trees. I was in Heaven, or at least I thought this must be what Heaven feels like. Being alone in the silence of the mountains was very comforting to me. When it was just me on a slope, and all I could hear was the swoosh of my skis against the powdery snowscape, I felt one with my surroundings. It seemed so easy to access this energy, but there were far fewer distractions back then.

Many years have passed since those carefree days in the Rockies. I have evolved into my fabulous fifties, experienced a 14-year marriage, divorce, raising a son, years of singlehood and dating in midlife, cultivated a thriving therapy practice, built a second marriage to the love of my life, and challenged myself to grow and expand and develop courage. Along the way, I have deepened this connection to Spirit as Nature and God is Love. I have come to appreciate the importance of having this connection to access and return to my Self.

Through my personal experience and witnessing others in their spiritual discovery process, I strongly sense that there is a cooperative relationship with the Universe available to all who wish to connect with it. I refer to my connection more often now as my "spiritual source." It is an energy that I can plug into at any time.

When plugged into Source, which is within me (rather than seeking something outside of myself to plug into for energy, knowledge, clarity, wisdom, or support), I am empowered at the highest level. I can accomplish anything that I set my mind to as well as remain authentic, in integrity, and filled with courage to evolve and grow into the fullest expression of my true Self. For me, this fundamental relationship is what I was put on this planet

14

to share, teach, and learn, and is what fuels me with a sense of purpose. I also know deep in my bones that I am not alone, even if I am with myself, and this energy is available to me 24/7/365, even when I forget to plug into it.

I know these issues go beyond me as I have spent countless hours in my office speaking with folks I work with about their spiritual resources and connection, or lack thereof. When they are stuck, the missing link is usually a spiritual connection. We often explore what that is for them and how to strengthen it as they seek to reconnect with their own innate intuition and wisdom. Connecting with something greater tends to make the world seem less daunting and lonely.

Sometimes, we need to weed through layers of religious teachings or early conditioned programming that feels disempowering and limiting. Occasionally, those teachings serve as resources to reconnect and build a bridge back to faith. But anytime that genuine connection is encountered, beyond the programmed conditioning, the experience is consistent, although the words and descriptions may vary slightly. The experience is always described as feeling safe, supported, and loved unconditionally. Many often refer to it as pure love, as my grandmother did.

Do you have a connection like that? If not, would you like to develop one? If so, would you like to feel more connected or strengthen your practice? Are you ready to let go of feeling so alone and overwhelmed? You deserve to have all of your personal power available to you and to see life clearly from the vantage point of infinite choices. Life is abundant when you can open your Self to receive all that is available. You are never alone and have so much access to an unlimited supply of love and connection within you. When you are plugged in and connected to this deep knowing and trust that it is always there, joy and peace become your innate way of being, even when life around you may deliver unpredictable or chaotic events.

I am excited to share what I have learned and connected with along the way, trusting that something will inspire you to develop or deepen your own connection to how you understand and connect to Spirit. I also hope to empower you to feel more connected within our distractible, often disconnected world where so much information is coming at you and invite you to take some time to go within yourself, to the infinite source that exists within your own inner landscape to remember what you came to Earth to learn, share, and teach. Purpose is not always meant to be illuminated on a global scale. It is often best expressed in our day-to-day moments: a kind word, a hug, or a simple acknowledgment or act of kindness. As you continue to cultivate this precious and beautiful connection, you will begin to reveal a gorgeous garden of your soul overflowing with more love, deeper peace, broader joy, and infinite abundance.

I am here to walk with you every step of the way. Ready to begin?

Chapter 2

What Inhibits Your Connection?

I'm drowning. I'm drowning. I'm drowning.

This message continued to scream at me from inside my head as I sat in the pew toward the back of the church sanctuary, held my face in my hands, and cried uncontrollably. I was participating in a class at the church I was attending at the time, and that night, we were visiting the sanctuary. Church elders were up front, offering to pray with those who requested it. People would periodically put their hand on my back and encourage me, but I felt stuck to my seat. I finally mustered the courage to walk up and ask for prayers. The people were very sweet, and the words were comforting, but I still didn't feel clear and struggled to trust their words as they were other humans and not God. It was 2007, and I felt so out of control, lost, overwhelmed, and for the first time in my thirty-four years of being on this planet, I had no idea what the next step in my life would be.

The big decision on the table was whether or not to have a second baby. I was with my first husband then, and we had our son, who had turned three. I was overwhelmed with motherhood, taking care of a house that was way more than we could handle, and experienced a lack of partnership in parenting with my husband. We had been discussing having a second child since my son was born, and it was coming to a head. We had recently moved into a large house and were on track according to the "traditional life script" of school, degrees, marriage, starter house, jobs, kid, and a bigger house. Now it was time to add that second child to make the "perfect life" and the "perfect family," right? At least, that is what the dream I held in my head told me. I had always pictured myself with two children—a boy and a girl—hosting holidays and creating a home where our families would gather and enjoy family traditions and other traditional family events. My mother had done such an amazing job of creating that experience for us growing up that I figured I would follow in her footsteps. But things weren't turning out according to my seemingly perfect plan.

My pregnancy journey was high-risk and had been far from perfect. Although my son had become my world, and I wouldn't have traded him for anything, my day-to-day experience of motherhood was disillusioning, to say the least. Trying to care for a large house, pool, yard, and toddler was overwhelming for me. I also thought my husband and I would continue to grow together on this journey that we had set out on twelve years prior and that his idea of family was the same as mine. Somewhere along the way, in my naïve young mind, I forgot to ask him this. Once we had come this far, I realized that we were on two totally different pages, and this dream I had held was a fantasy. My reality was proving to be very different.

These inconsistencies between my current reality and my childhood dreams contributed to an internal battle, and I was forever criticizing myself. Deep in my heart, I didn't want another baby, but I was terrified to state that out loud. When I was brutally honest with myself, I wasn't sure if I even liked the life we had worked so hard to build, and I wondered why I was pulling into myself more and more and distancing myself emotionally and sexually from my husband. I felt guilty for feeling that way, for not wanting to fulfill this life script, and for not being able to provide this baby for my husband or even my son, who I was convinced would do better with a sibling. I also felt shame that although I loved my son more than life itself, I didn't love the responsibility of motherhood as much as I thought I would. I held a belief that because I didn't work as much as my husband and I was the primary parent at home, I should be able to handle most of this on my own. Why did I think I needed more from my husband? Wasn't his providing a stable income for us enough? I was stuck in ambivalence:

> *Should I have another baby? Should I follow my instinct and not have one? Is my instinct fear or intuition? Why don't I want to do this? What is wrong with me? I should want this. I always dreamed of having two children. Why am I giving up now? Why don't I like this more? Maybe I should just let fate decide. What if I can't do it? What if this next pregnancy is not safe and becomes life-threatening? Should I have another baby, or should I just give up? Or, for the first time in my life, am I willing to go against the grain and totally honor my own inner knowing?*

I felt utterly alone.

The real problem was that I was not in tune with my inner knowing enough to trust it. I felt disconnected from my intuition. I had lost track of my journaling practice, which is where I always felt closest to God, and I was spiraling into depression and anxiety, although, as a trained therapist, I wouldn't let myself own those diagnoses. I would tell myself I should know better, and I certainly should know how to fix this. When I finally returned to my journal and began to assess my current mindset after being gone from journaling for four years, I ended my entry with, "This needs to be like a year of therapy, except I am both the therapist and the client. We'll see how it goes. Just writing this has made me tired. You are worth the work, Wend. You can do both. You HAVE to!"

Alas, I was unsuccessful in my impossible endeavor to be both my therapist and client. I began to seek answers outside of myself. I read books on meditation, self-care, healing, and relaxation. I read more books on parenting and marriage, went to church, and got our son baptized. I asked a therapist friend for help and talked with my friends and family incessantly about my unhappiness. I had conversations with my husband about what was wrong with me and how I was going to try and fix myself, yet I never once looked at how far from myself I had strayed and how abandoned I felt on the inside or the seemingly-at-the-time preposterous idea that maybe my husband played a part as well. How had I gotten here? How had I drifted so far from my center?

The more life moved forward, and we continued to reach for "the next thing" to finally reach happiness, peace, and more connection, the more miserable I felt. I eventually landed on a decision not to have a second baby. But that only revealed a deeper conflict regarding my marriage as a whole. My husband agreed to honor my decision but carried resentment about his own personal dream not being fulfilled, among other things that were deteriorating our marriage and that we were not being honest with each other about.

By 2009, I was completely lost. I felt like my soul was dying on the inside. I knew that meditation and prayer would be helpful tools, but I consistently resisted them and continued to seek answers outside myself. I even went back to yoga but focused more on the physical practice than the spiritual benefits. I felt increasingly lost, more and more angry and resentful, and more and more overwhelmed. Depression was lurking in the background. I had faith, but I wasn't listening to the still, small voice inside me that was calling for me to come within. I believed that the answer lay in "just keep going" and eventually hoped that I would find peace and joy in the state my life had become.

But that never happened. Those years were spent locked in that place of indecision and ambivalence, trying to figure out the right decision and, once I had made one, thinking about how to make peace with that eventual decision. Internally, I continued to deteriorate.

Knowing what to do or learning about what I could do was not the answer I needed. This knowledge and learning gave me insight, but it did not help me put into practice all that I was taking in. We need to practice what we are learning in order to bring our lives into a different state. I had so many feelings during that confusing time, but I was resisting them rather than being willing to get close to them and actually move *through* them. I was so afraid of what I might find if I did. What if I didn't like what I found? What if that internal discovery sent me on a path that would turn my whole life upside down? Then what?

I know now that if I could have given myself permission to move through those feeling states of confusion, loneliness, guilt, shame, anxiety/fear, depression/sadness, etc., I would have encountered the other side of those experiences, which held the possibilities for relief, stability, clarity, and connection. But I continued to resist, and the feelings continued to persist. The fear that I had of turning my life upside down was very real.

Ultimately, when I finally did acknowledge myself in the matrix of my confusion, what I discovered was that I was not the inherent problem in my life. My marriage was. This epiphany ultimately guided me toward a divorce, which completely turned my life upside down and right side up simultaneously. It was the most devastating and liberating decision I had ever made. But the good news was that I had finally reconnected with my Self and was beginning once again to feel guided by something greater than me.

"So, I was listening to this podcast . . ." "I'm following this person on Instagram . . ." "I read this quote on Facebook . . ." "I watched this video on YouTube . . ." "I saw this thing on TikTok . . ." and on and on and on. I hear these words in my office every day. Beyond my personal experience, as a society, we have become very preoccupied with taking in information. We spend endless hours seeking a solution to our current state of disconnection. Yet rather than taking the time to use the meditations provided in the videos, work through the exercises that this expert or influencer offers more than once, or root these new ideas into our daily habits, we move on to the next promise of instant transformation and settle into the belief that we have tried everything and there is no way out. From that space, we may choose to avoid our experience altogether by numbing ourselves with substances: sex, sugar, shopping, and/or scrolling through social media.

Have you ever heard yourself whisper, "What is wrong with me that I can't seem to have the beautiful life everyone else seems to have so easily?" The more we seek outside, the more disconnected we become. We have more knowledge but feel more chaotic than ever. People come into my office feeling restless, discontented, frustrated, angry, lost, lonely, overwhelmed, and anxious with no idea why, despite their diligent efforts to research a solution, they feel so stuck. Why is it so hard?

You will hear me repeat this over and over. It is so hard because the answers are *not outside of you*. They are within you. Spending time inside yourself can sometimes be scary. Many folks say to me, "I don't know what I would do if I had to actually spend time inside my head. I spend most of my time trying to steer clear of that mess!" So, what keeps you from connecting to the promises of love, joy, peace, and abundance discussed in Chapter 1? Let's take a look at some of the obstacles that get in your way and send you seeking outside yourself for "the solution," "the answer," "the quick fix," "the next best thing," or "the instant transformation."

What Disconnects You From **LOVE**?

- *Feeling Alone, Lonely, or Isolated* – Have you ever been in a relationship and felt lonely? Nothing is more painful than when you are with someone in a relationship where you are supposed to feel love and connection, and you feel more disconnected and lonely than if you were single. Or, if you are single and feel disconnected from the world around you because you work from home, don't have the social connections you would like to have, or feel like you just don't fit into the world anymore. As a human being, you were created to connect with others, but many times, with online culture, you might lack opportunities to connect in person and lose track of how to relate to others in a way that fosters love and connection. You may also feel desensitized to humanity due to so much stimulation about the world's polarization, destruction, and violence. It's easy to feel like you are the only one in your experience and wonder if anyone would really understand you.

- *Myths about Love and Connection* – Getting caught up in the messaging around love and connection is easy: that others are here to make you happy, that it is your responsibility to make everyone else happy, and that making someone happy is the same as loving them. Or you might think that a partner is here to meet all of your needs or is supposed to help you manage your emotional state or your life in general. These myths tend to block out your ability to experience love more deeply or to understand what it truly means to love someone. Also, when you constantly abandon yourself, lie to yourself, and/or betray yourself, you may tend to project that out onto others but call that love.

- *Seeking Outside Yourself for Love Before You Have Discovered It Within* – This has become a cliché statement and is common to say. However, it is true. If you think that someone else will be able to love you when you don't even love yourself, you will be sorely disappointed or, at the very least, highly confused about why you continue to attract toxic relationships.

- *Plugging Into the Wrong Source* – If you are plugging into another person for your life force, energy, or love, you will eventually drain them of all of their energy. If someone is plugging into you and calling that love, you will eventually be drained. You are in the wrong relationship if either of these things is occurring. This is what toxic relationships are made of. It is easy to get the message that another person is the answer to your suffering, but this is a highly dysfunctional myth about relationships. You must first plug into your spiritual source—the true source of your life force—and then you can send energy to another person. If both partners are giving and receiving from this space, no one is drained; both parties remain filled up and give from the overflow.

- *Unhealed Trauma* – When you have avoided or suppressed/repressed wounds from the past, you may have constructed protective mechanisms to cope or survive your experience. These coping mechanisms often form walls to keep others out and may even keep you from accessing the pain required to heal, thus keeping you stuck in old dysfunctional patterns and sealed off from healthy love.

- *Religious Abuse/Trauma/Limiting Dogma and Rules* – If you grew up in a strict religious household or an extremely narrow tradition, you may struggle to receive love or believe that you are truly deserving of love if you are less than perfect. You might even believe that you are inherently flawed or damaged. Or you may have experienced religious authority figures who violated and abused their authority in the name of God. Or you were taught to believe that God is angry, jealous, and potentially violent if you should venture outside the lines or that you simply don't belong in God's family. These beliefs can limit your ability to receive love and may even interfere with your ability to trust in the potential to foster a different spiritual relationship.

What Limits Your **JOY**?

- *Feeling Stuck and Resisting Growth and Change* – When you're stuck, you feel limited, caged, and hopeless. Joy becomes an afterthought when you feel lodged in quicksand. It is problematic from this vantage point to know where to begin. Sometimes, considering change can feel like too big of a task, and venturing into the unfamiliar does not seem appealing even though you are suffering. Staying with the familiar, even when uncomfortable, tends to be the go-to state for most folks. This is when I tend to hear the response of "Yes, but . . ." when I offer a way out of the darkness. "Yes, but I tried that already, and it didn't work." "Yes, but I don't have the time to dedicate to myself." "Yes, but who is going to take care of my kids?" "Yes, but those are such simple solutions. Surely, it is going to take more than breathing to move me from this place!"

- *Too Much Do-ing and Not Enough Be-ing* – Mainstream culture is obsessed with doing. Always moving from here to there with endless to-do lists, activities to attend to, places to shuttle your children, or commitments asked of you that you said "Yes" to when you secretly wanted to say "No." When this imbalance occurs, and you are stuck in a *doing* cycle without any room to *be*, your joy is drained. It may feel exciting to feel so needed at first, but eventually, you will wonder, "When do I get a turn to rest?"

- *Ambivalence* – This is the frozen state of indecision. As I described in my story earlier, you get caught in a loop of "Should I do this? Or should I do that? But if I do this, then this might happen. And if I do that, then that might happen. What is the right answer? Who can tell me what to do? How will I know if I'm making the right decision? Which sign is the right one to follow?" This typically occurs when what you *want* to do conflicts with what you believe you *should* do. You keep hoping that you will get okay with the "shoulds," but eventually, this wears down your ability to feel authentic in your life and keeps you in a constant state of avoidance and confusion. There is nothing like feeling like an imposter in your life to rob you of your joy.

- *Forgetting You Are a Spiritual Being Having a Human Experience* – When you forget, you abandon yourself. You get lost in the external pull toward what seem like "answers" without the tools needed to litmus those answers against your Truth. This is what keeps you searching and makes you feel so lost. When you are untethered from your Self, joy is a distant wish.

What Interferes with Your **PEACE**?

- *Anxiety and Depression* – When you are too focused on the past and what you "woulda, shoulda, coulda" done, depression sets in. When you are too focused on the future and the "what ifs," anxiety shows up. When you are too far behind or too far forward, you feel "off." You might feel restless or discontent. You might wonder what is wrong with you or what you must do to stop it. These states are the opposite of peace; continuing to move in either direction exacerbates your suffering.

- *Overwhelm* – You may struggle with feeling like there are so many people pulling on you, the list of responsibilities on your plate is never-ending, and there is never enough time. You may feel suffocated at times by how your life has evolved and sometimes feel as though you can't breathe, let alone catch your breath. You are stuck in a state of survival and chaos that makes peace seem impossible.

- *Distraction* – How many times a day do you check your phone? How many emails flood your inbox? How many people in your life rely on you for their life management? How many offers do you get to *do* something? How many chores still need to be done? The list goes on and on. We live in a distracted world with constant options for doing anything but what actually serves us. This leads you to feel scattered and stretched thin and running on fumes. How peaceful is that?

- *The Incessant Drive to Figure it Out* – In this world of information overload and Google, there exists an illusion that you can figure anything out. You may feel pulled to have the answers to know things beyond your scope of knowledge and/or training, and surely, if you spend enough time researching, reading, or gathering data or watching enough YouTube, you can understand it and be able to feel like you have a rationale that makes sense. However, some things are not meant to be figured out. They are meant to be experienced or known. This comes more from a right-brain process than a left-brain process. Figuring it out just becomes another distraction and leads you to avoid whatever message the current situation is trying to help you get in touch with. This ends up leading you further away from the peace you seek rather than drawing you closer to it.

What Blocks Your **ABUNDANCE?**

- *Limited Thinking* – Maybe you believe that you can only have or receive so much before it becomes "too much." This comes from beliefs that you are not enough, that you are unworthy of all that life has to offer you, that you are not valuable enough, lovable enough, or that you cannot possibly have everything you wish for. These thoughts and beliefs limit you and keep you closed off from your full potential. It keeps your life small.

- *Perfectionism* – The more perfect you try to make your life, the more imprisoned you will become. Nothing ever feels like enough; your expectations become limiting, and when you always seek to make everything perfect, you may tend to procrastinate the things that would bring more love, joy, and peace into your life. Perfectionism is also a form of limited thinking because there is only one option for your experience: perfect. And the fact that this is not possible keeps you stuck in a constant state of disappointment, shame, and guilt. It is very difficult to expand from there.

- *Focus on Lack or What Doesn't Work or What You Don't Have* – You may have heard the saying, "What you focus on expands." When your focus is on what you don't have, what you wish you had, what is not working, or what is missing, you will tend to get more of those things. Most of us are great at complaining and being vocal about what we don't like about ourselves or our lives. When asked to list your strengths, you may struggle with this. Although you constantly seek solutions, this inherently implies that you, your life, or those around you are problems. The focus is on what is wrong rather than what is right. When I encourage you to focus on what is right in your life, I'm not talking about the Pollyanna principle of positivity. I'm talking about being realistic with the full spectrum of your experience.

Mary came into my office as she was struggling in her marriage. She was stuck and wondering if her marriage was salvageable and if she was salvageable. This woman, who was beautiful on the outside, high-achieving, intelligent, and extremely capable of managing the majority of her complex life without the support of a partner, felt lifeless, confused, lonely, lost, and disconnected from herself. She had also begun to suffer physical symptoms of pain and dysphoria that no doctor could explain. "I just don't know what's wrong with me. I don't even feel like I'm a person anymore. I'm so lost, and I just don't know what to do. My husband said I needed to come to therapy to work on myself."

When I asked if her husband would be willing to join her, she replied, "No, he doesn't believe in therapy, and besides, he says I am the problem, so why would he need to come?" She added, "My husband was so amazing at the beginning of our relationship. I had never felt a love like that. I was his everything, and he was mine. I just don't know what I did that made it all change. I keep hoping that one day, the man I married will return. I just know that I can't keep going on like this. I'm miserable."

Mary shared that shortly into the marriage, things began to turn, and her husband began to ask things of her that she was uncomfortable with. He became jealous of her friends and critical of her appearance and life choices. She began doubting herself and surrendered her intuition and power to her husband and his needs.

Coming to therapy was Mary's first step toward acknowledging the nudge within her that she needed to change something. She had no idea what that would be or what life might look like once she stepped forward, but she knew she couldn't continue on the current path. She felt as if she were dying on the inside. Even though your situation may differ from Mary's, does her experience sound familiar?

When I asked Mary what she wanted for herself, she immediately reacted with, "What do you mean?" So we began there. I asked Mary to start observing her inner state when she was engaged in her life at home and how she felt during specific interactions with her husband. I gave her the tool to close her eyes and go within herself to tune into what she was feeling, where those feelings live in her body, and any messages she began to notice may be attached to those sensations. I also suggested journaling as a way to tune into her inner self-talk around her beliefs about herself. Lastly, we added for her to choose one activity she could begin implementing that was for her and not for anyone else. She said she had always wanted to take a yoga class but was afraid that if she took the time, her husband or children would suffer and complain that she was neglecting their needs. But she was willing to try it out and see what happened.

Over the next several months, as Mary began to put these tools into practice, she began to look a bit brighter, spoke with a bit more confidence and clarity, and once again saw herself as a

31

person who mattered. She began engaging in more self-care, learning boundaries, and strengthening her ability to tune into herself and her intuition. She started reclaiming her life. Through her yoga and journaling practices, she once again discovered a spiritual connection that reminded her that she was important, precious, and lovable, just as she is. She also became aware that her marriage was toxic and began building the strength within her to confront this reality and challenge the relationship.

Without going within, Mary would have continued to search outside herself for the solution to her shame and suffering, including looking to me as her therapist for what she needed to do. Within herself, she began to accept that nothing was actually wrong with her except that she was absorbing the toxicity of her marriage and making the problems she and her husband were facing all about her. As Mary began to slow down and tune in, she tapped into the consciousness within her and plugged back into her spiritual source. Once that connection occurred, she began to get unstuck, see more possibilities, feel more joy, and open space to feel love in a whole new way. More days than not, she began to feel less pain in her body. As she distanced herself from the chaos of toxic dynamics, she began to experience moments of peace and realized that she had so many more choices available to her than the suffering she had felt imprisoned by for so long.

Have you ever felt stuck and lost? Searching for solutions everywhere else but within you? Do you struggle to make time for yourself amid the incessant pulls on your time and energy? Maybe you've been trapped in ambivalence regarding an important life decision or awakened to the reality that a relationship is draining the life out of you.

It is easy to forget and lose track of our center. Most of the folks I work with start in that place. I know I have cycled through different forms of these feelings at various times in my life. I drift into a space of "forgetting" as if I have gone to sleep and eventually wake up and "remember" that the wisdom I seek or the connection I am yearning for is spiritual more than physical or intellectual. This is part of being human.

Our left brain seeks to understand and figure out life and the "why" behind experiences. It operates with words, facts, numbers, and concrete evidence. It also contains the ego or personality that tends to make comparisons, find differences, and holds all the coping mechanisms and defenses you established to survive your childhood.

Our right brain functions are underutilized. This is where symbols, dreams, subconscious and unconscious material, music, imagination, and other less concrete functions reside. This aspect of our brain allows us to connect with something beyond our physical form, tap into our higher states of consciousness, and celebrate a sense of oneness with all things in the Universe. This is the part of the brain we utilize when we talk more about spiritual concepts.

Our Western culture values the left brain as a dominant function of what defines a powerful human being. Due to this imbalance, you may often get caught in the cycle of going unconscious, enduring suffering, and eventually seeking some end to your suffering, only to discover that the answer is nowhere to be found outside yourself. You must go within. Most religious traditions will ultimately send you inside yourself to spend time with God. Even Jesus went into the garden by himself to meditate and pray. So, it makes sense that you might not instinctually seek to connect with Spirit within you that is formless, timeless, beyond labels, and enigmatic because why on earth would you think that type of thing would be an authority on anything?

The interesting concept here is that by going within to seek that connection to something greater than yourself—that is, both you and everything else around you—your concept of authority moves from an external authority to an internal authority about you and your life. It also challenges you to access the wisdom of your right brain, which houses this way of experiencing or *be-ing* in your life. When you connect with Spirit within you, you access a power so much greater than your limited ego-mind can conceptualize. You expand your mind, literally, and begin to use a more balanced approach to connection. Greater consciousness reveals infinite choices and thus allows you to expand beyond your limited beliefs and grow into a life with unlimited love, joy, peace, and abundance. The Universe offers possibilities beyond your imagination, and it only requires that you connect with this energy and participate in the flow of giving and receiving, asking and answering, to experience that cooperative relationship.

This connection is available to anyone who seeks it. It is always present and never absent. You can use the tools discussed in the upcoming chapters to cultivate and embody this connection in your daily living. At first, you will need to be more intentional in your practice. As you continue to integrate this connection more into your life, it will feel very accessible and require less effort to plug in. It doesn't mean you won't encounter life phases where you may forget occasionally, but it will take you less time to return to yourself. Because once you sense what this supportive connection feels like, you will yearn for it when it feels distant. You will seek it when it feels lost. And you will crave it when you are suffering.

When life is good, and you are celebrating the promises, you will also return to this connection to share gratitude and appreciation for how the Universe supports you. It will become like an old friend whom, even when time goes by between contact, you can pick back up as if no time has passed. This presence is always here for you. The only thing that changes is that you turn away from it. But as soon as you turn back toward it, it is right there for you. And that is also why you are never alone, as my parents taught me when I was young. This presence or energy is always around you whether or not you are conscious of it or plugged into it. It's right there. The easiest place to plug in is within you. With one simple breath, close your eyes and sense it.

Spirit *is*. When we are still, we feel it. The Bible references this in Psalm 46:10: "Be still and know that I am God." When you can trust in the never-ending presence of Spirit, you can lean into the support and know you are not alone. The Fray's song "Be Still" expresses this sentiment beautifully. I encourage you to listen and soak in the message.

Let's end with a Sanskrit prayer from the Anusara Yoga tradition; it is used as an invocation for practice. This prayer is often sung, and these types of prayers will be explored further in Chapter 6, where I discuss music and mantras. Feel free to look up a version of this invocation on your favorite music platform, *Tejase* or *Anusara Invocation*. It is a gentle reminder of the connection I will be helping you cultivate. As you continue to read and gain sight of your path toward this sacred connection, may you once again recall that your True Nature is Spirit, and you have unlimited access to all the blessings in the Universe.

Sanskrit:
Om Namah Shivaya Gurave
Saccidananda Murtaye
Nisprapancaya Shantaya
Niralambaya Tejase

English:
I bow to the presence of the Divine within, Our true and highest teacher
That lives in and around us as Being, Consciousness, and Bliss,
It is ever-present and radiates peace,
Lighting the way to transformation.

~ from the Anusara Teacher Training Manual

Chapter 3

Tools for Cultivating Your Path

Now that you are more clear and understand what gets in your way, let's talk about how you can cultivate your connection. The good news is that you *can* go within to discover and connect with the promises of love, joy, peace, and abundance. I have listed seven tools for you that are conduits of connection. You will have a direct plug into your Source when you practice these tools. As you continue to practice and integrate these tools, you will begin to build a strong relationship that supports you through anything that life throws your way. You can return to these tools anytime and have immediate access to your connection and the wisdom within that connection. I have personally used all seven tools and integrated them into my personal practice. I don't use them *all* simultaneously, but I interchangeably utilize what I need at different times and often use a combination of two or three.

These are not complex ideas and are easy to access and implement. Having a space to meditate, journal, or pray is helpful but not required. I know many busy moms who meditate in their closets—it seems to be the one place no one looks for them! Some tools you can integrate as a regular part of your daily life, and some you will have to carve out time for. The more I integrate and use these tools, the more my life flows and expands in ways I never could have imagined.

As we move into the following chapters, I will go into depth for each tool presented below. I will share my own story and the stories of others. The more you lean into this connection, the more your life will evolve into more love, joy, peace, and abundance than *you* could have ever imagined.

Tool #1: Journaling – A Dialogue with the Divine

Journaling is typically the first thing I recommend to those I work with when they begin therapy. It seems cliché, and I will often hear, "Please don't tell me to just journal. That doesn't really do anything for me." However, journaling is not only a way to give the thoughts in your head a place to go but can also serve as a way to dialogue with the divine and connect with your Higher Self. Once you begin to write, oftentimes, you may start to gain clarity within a confusing situation, or a new thought is inspired that was not present before you started writing. When you review your entry, you might wonder who wrote those words. It's as if your conscious mind can let go, and a greater consciousness, a divine consciousness, can flow through you onto the pages. Journaling is the umbrella tool for all the other tools listed because it can be used on its own, but it also serves as a perfect companion to any of the other tools.

Tool #2: Prayer – Start the Conversation

Prayer is a way to speak to God. It starts the conversation. Anne Lamott authored an amazing book on prayer titled *Help, Thanks, Wow: The Three Essential Prayers.* That beautifully sums up the primary themes of prayer. You may need help with something and wish to request assistance. You may want to express gratitude for what has happened or for the support. Or, when you are overwhelmed with the miracles in your life, you can express your joy, wonder, and devotion in prayer. In Chapter 5, I will share many different types of prayer and how my relationship with this practice has evolved from the simple prayer I shared at the beginning of this book.

Tool #3: Meditation – Listen for the Knowing

Meditation is the *listening.* Once you have put out your prayer, the part you may forget is to stop talking and be quiet. Here is where you can listen for any wisdom that comes to you. This is usually the "answer" you have been seeking or, at the very least, a deeper level of clarity. However, it may not come through in the words you are expecting and may not sound like you. You may get an impression or a "knowing," or a symbol, image, word, or phrase may come to mind. You may begin to decipher the difference between your "voice" and the "voice" of something greater and wiser than what you usually think of as *you.*

My prayer usually begins as some type of anxious rant or paragraph of questions, worries, thoughts, fears, etc. When I sit and listen, I may get a simple answer like, "Slow down," "Stop," or "Keep moving." When I struggled through the year my son was graduating from high school, and I was preemptively mourning the loss of him leaving home, the message was, "Release the goodbyes." The beauty of these messages is that they may not always make logical sense at first, but once you sit with them and allow them to percolate into your consciousness, they make more sense. For me, "releasing the goodbyes" was about saying goodbye to the many layers of memories of my son's growing up and giving myself permission to grieve and release each piece I was letting go of as the year went on.

In the book *Eat, Pray, Love*, Elizabeth Gilbert lies on the bathroom floor sobbing and pleading for God to tell her what to do amidst her desperate suffering in a lifeless marriage. At that moment, the simple message was, "Go back to bed, Liz." By trusting in this simple wisdom of the present moment, her connection with her inner knowing grew and ultimately led her on a pilgrimage to create a strong foundation upon which she built a much deeper knowing of herself and a pathway to discover who she was meant to be.

Tool #4: Yoga – Breathe In/Breathe Out

Yoga is the perfect form of a moving meditation. The physical practice of postures or *asanas* is the typical way we think about yoga, but many aspects of yoga can inform your connection to Spirit. When I went through my yoga teacher training program with Kripalu, I learned that there are eight limbs of yoga, and *asana* is merely one of those limbs. I will expand on these more in Chapter 8 but will summarize the other seven limbs briefly and simply here: *yama:* how you behave with others; *niyama:* how you behave toward yourself; *pranayama:* the breath; *pratyahara:* going within; *dharana:* intense concentration; *dhyana:* state of meditation; and *samadhi:* state of oneness.

Yoga is an all-encompassing path to spiritual connection. However, combining it with other tools can build a comprehensive connection that supports you in every way.

When you choose to practice yoga on a mat, coming back to your mat can become a microcosm for how you choose to live your life, and the lessons gained *on your mat* can then be taken back out into your life and practiced *off the mat.*

Tool #5: Music and Mantras – Calling in Spirit

Music is a large part of my spiritual practice. As you may have noticed in my references throughout this book, I have always found inspiration in songs, lyrics, and melodies. I often encourage folks I work with to make a playlist when they are struggling, as music speaks to the right brain and usually allows you to access deeper feelings your conscious mind may be defending you from feeling. "Call-and-response" music or spiritual songs are integrated into all religious traditions. In India, there is a type of call-and-response chanting called *kirtan.* I was first exposed to this during my hypnotherapy training program to "call in" and connect with Spirit before we began our day of learning. These chants were in Sanskrit, a language I did not understand, yet when I would sing the words, I felt a connection as if I had melted into God's presence. I felt like I had returned home. Using music, chanting, or other mantras (words or phrases that you repeat over and over as a way of calming your incessant mind-chatter and creating space to connect deeper within) are a fun and creative way to cultivate your spiritual connection and can be a great way to expand your spiritual practice beyond traditional methods.

Tool #6: Ritual and Ceremony – Anchor Your Connection

Ritual is perhaps my favorite form of spiritual connection. I use it for everything I wish to mark as important, to define a transition, celebrate a transformation, prepare for something new, or even complete something that has been a test of the soul.

41

Ritual helps to anchor your connection, honor an experience as sacred, and remember that this journey you are on in this lifetime is a sacred event. Ritual can be a way of inviting and honoring Spirit as your guide. It also helps you to anchor the knowing that you are not alone and that there is a greater energy surrounding and supporting every move you make along your path. It is a relationship that you are cultivating, and ritual helps to strengthen that relationship.

Ritual often has a bad reputation associated with misunderstandings about pagan traditions or even more negative associations with cults and darkness. That is not what I am referring to. I want to expand this viewpoint. There are rituals embedded in every religious tradition and culture. They mark time and rites of passage and celebrate how we evolve through life: birth, achievements, coming together, splitting apart, death, and anything else that might be deemed important.

Anchoring your connection with a ritual or ceremony becomes rooted in your memory and acts as a bookmark for that experience. I will share many examples in Chapter 9 that will help you relate to this concept and begin to imagine your own way of implementing ritual and ceremony in your life.

Tool #7: Nature: Spirit is Everywhere and in Everything

As I mentioned in the preface, my first connection to God was in the trees, the leaves, the mountains, and the natural elements surrounding me. I felt the presence of love before I even knew how to name it. I felt safe in nature, and I felt the aliveness of the earth when its elements surrounded me. Nature is the most accessible conduit for spiritual connection because it is not associated with any religious tradition and, therefore, is a blank slate with no preconceived notions or ideas that you might have to sift through if you struggle with dysfunctional associations you may have picked up along the way. Nature is free. It is everywhere and does not require anything from you to connect with it. Most folks in my counseling office, if I ask them whether or not they have a spiritual connection, may initially say, "No," but when I ask them to come up with a symbol of support and connection, they will name "light," "the trees," "the ocean," "the mountains," or "the sun/moon/sky." And as I mentioned earlier, Spirit is everywhere and in everything. Nature allows you to both see and feel that by going outside your door.

As you continue to read, you will understand these tools on a deeper level and see clearly how to incorporate them into your life. Your goal with these tools is to create a "spiritual practice." I call it practice because you never master anything. There isn't anything to master here. It is simply a way of approaching each day with a willingness to learn and connect with your Source. It requires practice because it goes against much of what you may have been taught so far about how to go about finding relief for your suffering. These tools are ways to practice connecting. The more you practice, the more integrated your connection will become and the easier it will be to access the experiences of love, joy, peace, and abundance.

You are amazing and precious and messy and beautiful and so so so worthy of all that the Universe has to offer. I hope that as you continue to read and practice, you deepen your connection to the divine source of consciousness and wisdom within you and come to understand your inherent value. Standing in the truth of this value allows you to align your life with that understanding. May these tools charge up your connection and

43

provide you with access to a deeply powerful way of living that emits the brightest light to shine on those around you and inspire others to connect to their source and shine their light. May the Universe be filled with this light and bring the blessings of love, joy, peace, and abundance to us all!

Chapter 4

Journaling—A Dialogue with the Divine

I referred to my first journal as "a diary." It had a lock, and I wrote most of my entries in the bathroom late at night. I'm not sure why that felt like the best place to write. I was in elementary school and would write about my struggles with friends and anything else that might have been happening to me physically or at school. What I knew of diaries consisted of entries similar to those in the book *Are You There God? It's Me, Margaret* by Judy Blume. That book was my introduction to writing about my inner world, and a diary seemed as good a place as any to talk to God. I always felt like I was documenting important things, sharing my story for someone someday to read as my legacy, or letting God in on what I wanted to share. I liked the idea of writing down my private thoughts, and because it had a lock, I knew it was just for me, but ultimately it was between me and God.

Somewhere along the way, those early diaries got lost and were replaced by journals. Journaling became a regular practice for me in college. That was where I met Dr. Mary Hill, my women's studies professor, who taught me about writing and encouraged me to write in my own voice. She always said I wasn't the most technical writer, but there was something about my style that she loved. She consistently encouraged me. Her assignments for all her classes (of which I took nearly all) were weekly journal entries about what we were reading or studying. Then, there were the end-of-semester papers on a more in-depth topic. This began to get me in the habit of writing regularly. Soon, I was filling my own personal journals and sharing my experiences, struggles, inner thoughts, relationship drama, and anything else that would drift through my mind.

This practice soothed me, and I always felt clearer by the end of an entry than when I started. I continued to journal as I ventured out to Breckenridge and into the first few years of my first marriage. However, the more I became caught up in my marriage, and the more I became disconnected from myself, the less I wrote and the more I focused on things outside myself. Writing seemed to take a back seat.

Looking back now, I understand that the less I journaled, the further away from myself I would drift. I also now have a deeper understanding of my early relationship patterns, which consisted of me losing myself in the relationship with a disproportionate focus on my partner. The more focused I became on my partner, the less of *me* existed; thus, writing was almost an afterthought. Yet, my journal was always nearby, and frequently, I felt it calling to me like an old friend. But I would often feel too overwhelmed to even think about writing.

46

In those early days, I censored myself a bit more as it was tough for me to tell my entire truth, even to myself, about the dysfunction I was creating and experiencing in those relationships. Inevitably, something would shake me awake for a moment, or I would get confused, hurt, or unsure of where to turn, and I would seek out my journal again. Each time I wrote, it was as if I was coming home to myself, and I would wonder why I had waited so long. Here is an example of one of my many returns:

> *1:22 am ~ November 23, 1997 (the last entry before this was April 29, 1996)*

> *Well, here I am . . . can't sleep. I feel as if I have 5,000 thoughts racing around in my head, and I felt that I would scream unless I have a way to drain them out. Then, I remembered my journal, not the gratitude journal with five lines but my real journal, with the good paper, leather cover, and gold-lined pages. This and similar ones saved me once, so what better friend to call upon?*

At the time of this journal entry, I was twenty-four and living in a run-down apartment in "married housing" at the University of Florida in Gainesville. I had left home, gotten married, and moved to a foreign place where I was a fish out of water. I had started graduate school, and my husband was buried in the law school library, trying to learn how to think like an attorney. I was deeply struggling at the time with my family of origin. We were gradually making our way through the murky maze of codependency that had been hidden and dormant in our unconsciousness for several years. Having honest communication and healthy boundaries were new concepts for all of us, and we were very gradually healing and working our way toward a much more functional way of loving each other.

This particular night, I was struggling with many pieces of this puzzle that were coming to light, and I was beginning to understand how dysfunctional my family had been, but we just couldn't see it until now. I continued to write out my thoughts, and several pages later, I concluded the above entry with these words:

> *My family will never be able to truly understand the [internal] work I am doing. I think I even lose sight of it sometimes, and that can make me feel misunderstood and very alone. I need someone to share my work with! I need to process and share it with myself, I guess. I want to do that. I miss doing that. Instead of watching TV and making my brain race around, I need to write and talk to myself. What do I want out of this next phase of my life? I need to practice what I preach . . . "dialogue with myself." It's the only way to truly gain direction. If I unpack my emotional baggage here, I can make room for [my husband.] See, I know what I need to do. I always do. I just needed to clear away the clutter. Shit, I got cobwebs growing in my brain, I've pushed so much stuff away, and I'm adding tons of new stuff every day. I don't want to go through the motions of this experience in my life; I need to write it into life. Well, I've vented. Now Wend, put this away and let yourself rest. You deserve that, just relax. I love you very much! Love, Me*

I wrote two more entries over the next year and then did not write in that journal again. I must have gotten a new journal for Christmas because, in January 2002, I once again sat down to write. At that time, I was beginning a new life chapter of trying to get pregnant. I always documented the beginning and ending dates of my journals. The journal I started in 2002 took me seven years to fill and brought me to the cusp of deciding whether or not to leave my marriage. The years in between were repetitions

48

of the cycle of getting lost and then once again finding myself in my journaling.

In 2009, I began to write regularly once again. I wrote through my decision to get a divorce, through the divorce, and for the next twelve years after that, which included seven years of singlehood, raising my son as a single parent, dating in midlife, and eventually meeting my current husband and braving marriage once again. I filled eighteen journals during those years.

To say that journaling saved my life multiple times would be an understatement.

Journaling became a refuge where I talked to God, asked for help, listened to myself, honed my inner knowing, and got to know myself in a way that allowed me to heal so many dysfunctional patterns I had collected throughout my early life. The more I wrote, the more I felt the presence of Spirit all around me and the more connected to something deep and true within myself I became:

> *Sunday 10/9/2016 @ 7:26 am ~*
>
> *This is where I feel most connected these days—here in my journal. The connection flows through me and onto the page. What reflects back to me in my writings helps me to glimpse a bit more of my soul and how Divine energy comes through me. As I shared during dinner with (my friend) Allison last night, it came to me that I am currently very focused on my "interior." The outside life goes on, but the focus of my experience is primarily on the inside. Although I enjoy being outside in the fresh air, that is also a way of connecting and tuning into my inner purpose. I love just being quiet and listening to the sounds of the birds or the wind or water droplets. I love to watch the sunrise and how the colors in the sky emerge as the light of day increases.*

49

I had finally come home to myself! It took many years to decompress from the stress of a dysfunctional marriage, divorce, and raising a young son. But the more I continued to write, the more tuned into my Self (my spiritual Higher Self) I became, and the closer I felt to a presence much greater than me and to the cooperative nature of the Universe. As these entries evolve through time, you will likely sense my deepening understanding of these concepts.

I am forever grateful for that midlife intermission, allowing me space to reset and grow up and out of the embedded coping patterns I had developed as a little girl. But as you may also glean from my writings, I was returning to that same core being who fell in love with that poster her father bought her at five years old. We seem to go so far away from ourselves as we attempt to navigate life. But ultimately, our return is as George Elliot so beautifully described: "We shall not cease from exploration, and the end of all our exploring will be to arrive where we started and know the place for the first time."

I continued the journal entry from above:

> *I had inspiration for a blog titled: "Love and Relationships: The Great Mystery." I'm finding more fascination with the mystery of the soul and of how that Divine weaving occurs. There is so much creativity in that. How that is expressed through our individual inner workings and then between our connections within our relationships is what I am going to spend more time observing. The more I observe, the more I am fascinated. It's almost as if I am beginning to glimpse the energy currents that connect us all. It's like watching electric currents interchanging between two poles (like in one of those balls with all the electric charges/currents displaying themselves). It shows how we are all connected to and with EVERYTHING and that every thought, feeling, action, and*

intention is an energy exchange with the entire Universe. And therefore, it is important to recognize our own responsibility and participation in such exchanges.

Through this entry, I began to formulate my current philosophy on relationships. But without this time with myself, journaling all of my inner workings along the way, I would have had a much more difficult time arriving at such an understanding of the message I wanted to share.

During these years of introspection, I also practiced all the tools outlined in the rest of this book. This first tool provides a space to integrate all the other tools together. In your journal is your dialogue with the Divine, the place to process all that is happening for you, rest your prayers, record messages you receive in meditation, lessons you receive on your yoga mat, and other inspirations from music and nature. Journaling has brought forth many inspired ideas for rituals, some of which I will share in Chapter 9.

Journals can be love letters to God and the Spirit within you. They are also a great place to communicate with your inner child. You will hear the cries of your more innocent self, who may need something from you. The more you journal, the easier it becomes, and the more you will long for this time with yourself. Even if you don't think you are much of a writer or struggle to journal, just start. Write whatever is on your mind. Start by writing about your surroundings, as I did in this entry:

Tuesday 9/20/22 @ 11:38 am ~

"Just begin," says Julia Cameron in "The Right to Write." And so I begin where I am—at Kraft Azalea Park—drinking my green smoothie, feeling the gentler, cooler breeze that lets me know fall is here, and staring out at the beautiful water framed by oaks

and palms and tropical foliage. No leaves turning, but the lighter shade of green reminds me it is getting close to my birthday and more breathable days. Outside calls to me — we've been indoors for too long. I feel inspired and like I have been reunited with a long-lost love as I return here to my beloved journal and give myself permission and space and encouragement to write. I am here!

What has your experience been with journaling so far? In today's world, you may look to typing or speaking into your phone, keeping journal entries in your computer's folders, or using a journaling app. But I strongly encourage you to experiment with journaling the old-fashioned way with pen and paper. The act of physically writing out your thoughts is a form of release and also removes all energetic interference, allowing you to be a clear channel for a greater consciousness to flow through you. Give it a try. Use a journal that speaks to you. It may be a plain spiral notebook, or it may be ornate with inspirational quotes and beautiful artwork, or something in between. Whatever calls to you.

Then, on the first blank page of the journal or the inside cover, write the date of your first entry. I also like to write out my whole name, including the spiritual name I was given by a sacred teacher along my journey, and then state a type of intention for that journal or a summary statement of that current life chapter or something I wish to bring into my life. For example, inside the front cover of the journal from the excerpt above, the page reads:

Wendy Elizabeth Crane

"Ananda"

June 5, 2016 ~ December 4, 2016

Opening to Love … A New Chapter … with Patient Expectancy

Stating a type of intention for your journal helps you to see the space in your life those entries speak to. What is fascinating is that, although I had no way of predicting the future, this journal's entries were preparing me for the *next* life chapter because, in March 2017, I met my current husband. The love I was opening to, with patient expectancy, was right around the corner. Who knew? Well, I guess my Higher Self knew! This is why I trust this process so much. You are always being guided to exactly where you need to be. "Wherever you go, there you are," as Jon Kabat-Zinn preaches. Pretty cool, right? You don't know what is in store, but the more connected you are to your intuitive knowing, the more you will travel on the path of your highest good. Journaling is a significant tool to assist with this.

My wish for you is that you find a journaling practice that supports you in times that you need it and times that you need to remember yourself. Keep them for yourself. And when you forget or lose your way, pull out a past journal and re-read the entries. It will remind you where you have been, and you can gain perspective on how the Universe has supported you during those more challenging times. You will see how far you have come and your growth through different life chapters.

Journaling is also a wonderful way to become aware of patterns you cycle through and how long you may have been stuck in a downward spiral. If you aren't sure about a decision that you need to make, go back and read previous journal entries. If you were complaining about the same dynamics you are still writing about today, months or even years later, you may have more incentive to take that big step or risk to change your life.

Take your first step toward cultivating your spiritual connection and get yourself a journal today. Write what you see and experience, and begin to listen for your True Self and the voice of something greater than you to emerge. Permit yourself to make the connection you were looking for when you picked up this book. Let the messages flowing onto your pages speak to you. Then, as you read through the remaining chapters, choose other tools to combine with journaling and see how those combinations enhance your connection.

Chapter 5

Prayer—Start the Conversation

A s a young person, my favorite story was "Footprints in the Sand." If you are not familiar with it, or even if you are, read on:

One night, a man had a dream. He dreamed that he was walking along the beach with the Lord. Across the sky flashed scenes from his life. For each scene, he noticed two sets of footprints in the sand; one belonged to him and the other to the Lord.

When the last scene of his life flashed before him, he looked back at the footprints in the sand. He noticed that many times along his life's path, there was only one set of footprints. He also noticed that it happened at the very lowest and saddest times in his life.

This really bothered him, and he questioned the Lord about it. "Lord, you said that once I decided to follow you, you'd walk with me all the way. But I have noticed that during the most troublesome times in my life, there is only one set of footprints. I don't understand why, when I needed you most, you would leave me."

The Lord replied, "My precious, precious child, I love you, and I would never leave you. During your times of trial and suffering, when you see only one set of footprints, it was then that I carried you."

This story served as part of the foundation of my relationship with God but also as an inner knowing about my prayers and how they were being received by a Love that existed above and beyond everything else in my life. Even when I forgot, I would come back to the understanding that God was never far away and that I was being carried when the seas of life were unbearable. That often sent me to a place of total surrender, trusting that I was being held and would eventually arrive at a safe harbor, even when I had no idea what that would be or would look like. However, this practice was not always easy for me as a perfectionistic control freak who, most of the time, thought she was in charge of her life direction. But the feeling of surrender was so freeing that I continued to practice.

These days, when I reach that place, lying flat on the ground feels as good a place as any to rest in the energy that carries me. I have an altar in my home that houses many of my spiritual symbols and serves as a centralized location to access my connection. I will often sit or lie down in front of it, offer up the burdens I am trying to carry alone, and allow myself to relax into the support and love that are always here for me. I imagine being held in the palms of some very large hands or enveloped by large angel wings with the overarching knowledge that it is safe to rest.

Spirit is always here for you. It is always present and never absent. An effective way to connect with that energy is to engage in conversation. As I've already mentioned, prayer starts the conversation. As we will discuss in the next chapter, meditation is the listening. For me, prayer is often an attempt to surrender something I am holding too tightly to or a request to help me get clear. Most of the time, the idea of prayer comes to me when I'm at my wit's end; I have exhausted all outside sources, and the only place to turn is within to plug into a greater wisdom that knows much more than my human mind can muster on her own. It also comes to mind when I feel humbled by blessings in my life or abundance that shows up or when I feel exceptionally grateful. Honestly, prayer is so helpful and accessible that utilizing it sooner rather than later is highly recommended, but as humans, we often have to suffer a bit before we remember that we have tools and resources. I hope what I am sharing helps you remember sooner so that suffering is lessened.

In this chapter, you will encounter different examples of prayers you can use or expand upon as you develop your way of speaking with Spirit. These may help you generate inspiration for incorporating prayer into your spiritual practice and connect with your understanding of what the greater consciousness you are speaking with is comprised of.

As I shared in the preface, the Thank you, Lord prayer is a piece of my spiritual foundation and one I return to often when I want to express gratitude. The Serenity Prayer from the 12-step traditions is another go-to for me when I want to let go of control:

> *God grant me the serenity to accept the things I cannot change, the courage to change the things I can, and the wisdom to know the difference.*

When I want to remember my connection and what God means to me, I listen to a beautiful song by Sirgun Kaur, a woman from the Sikh tradition, titled "Amen." It describes a creative presence that is the source of everything in the universe and resides within every being, expressing itself through creativity. Forgiveness is a refuge from the suffering often generated in the world.

Kaur sings with such deep devotion that it feels intimate and cooperative. She celebrates her connection to the divine throughout the song with the word "hallelujah." For some reason, whenever I hear hallelujah, I want to cry. It elicits a primitive response from somewhere deep within my soul, calling out in surrender or a yearning to connect with God.

"Hallelujah" is a simple prayer in and of itself. Repeat softly to yourself now, "Hallelujah, hallelujah, hallelujah," and notice the response it evokes within you. Repeat it more loudly now and allow the vibrational frequency of this powerful word to resonate through your body. How does that feel?

Prayer does not have to be complex or formal. Your journal is also a wonderful place to write out your prayers. You can utilize formal prayers from religious teachings or simply include what is innately inspired from within you to become what can be a very casual conversation with the Divine.

Within my journal, I have my own way of conversing. These days, I end all my entries with this simple prayer of gratitude: *"Thank you, God, all the Angels and Benevolent Forces of the Universe for (insert whatever I want to express gratitude for) and all the blessings in my life. Thank you, thank you, thank you, thank you!"*

At the beginning of the coronavirus outbreak, when so many of us were scared and stay-at-home orders were becoming the norm, I was working through a program called A Course in Miracles (ACIM). I wrote the following prayer in my journal:

April 3rd, 2020 @ 3:50pm ~

God, I know that there is more going on here than we can imagine, and I trust in your energy of Love. I choose to surrender and rest in the love you provide and that you made in me. As the ACIM lesson for today states: "My fear attacks my invulnerability. Above all else, I want to see and to see differently. God is in everything I see because God is in my mind." Thank you for all the blessings, and I send love and light to anyone who is suffering or scared. I shine my light and love out into the world, AND I remember to fill myself first! The more I am full, the more light I can shine and share.

Nancy sat in my office in tears about her daughter, who was so lost in the world of drugs that she feared she would eventually die. Nancy had tried everything, even reaching out to famous television shows attempting to help families drowning in addiction. There were several attempts at rehab, meetings with police who had picked up her daughter on the street, sitting by a hospital bed after an overdose, and begging and pleading with her daughter when she would have brief moments of sobriety to choose life over this slow and painful road to death. Nancy felt helpless and hopeless and had completely lost herself in her attempts to save her daughter. "What do I do?" she asked, hoping I could offer a new solution that she had not yet tried. I understand that addiction is one of those circumstances that cannot be successfully intervened without a decision from the addict. At this point, Nancy was so drained of her life force from trying to "fix it" or "will it" to go away that she had nothing to offer. Rather than providing an answer full of therapeutic jargon or anything that minimized the sense of hopelessness that she felt, I offered for her to pray. I offered to send love and light to her daughter, wherever she was, and to call on a greater consciousness to watch over her and to guide her and their family to a space of what I like to refer to as "the highest good for all."

This highest good is not always what we humans think it should be. It doesn't always mean people won't die, get sick, or stay sick, or that everything has a happy ending and all the pain will go away. But it does mean that whatever happens is here for the growth of everyone involved, even those who aren't yet affected. This means that whatever happens is here to expand experiences and contribute to each person's purpose in this lifetime here on Earth.

This is not always easy or pleasant, but it allowed Nancy to rest her attempts at trying to carry her daughter's issues on her own shoulders all by herself. For Nancy and you, prayer provides an opportunity to release the burden, to give it over, and to invite in a presence much more powerful than you, with unlimited access to all the consciousness in the universe, to use whatever is happening to move closer to the highest good of all. This is where statements like "Let go, let God," "Get out of the way," and "Surrender to the Flow" come into play.

"I am going to commit to taking one full year to be with myself and abstain from dating," I announced to my mastermind group on a Wednesday morning in 2015, during the years between my divorce and meeting my current husband. I had been divorced for a little over five years, had experimented with dating, and had a couple of unsuccessful "situationships." I had become frustrated with my repetitious patterns of codependent interactions, attracting emotionally unavailable men, and it was all taking a severe toll on my heart. I was fed up. I was tired. And I was ready to take drastic measures. Through journaling, prayer, and meditation, I realized that taking a year off was necessary to integrate the beliefs and concepts I had learned through therapy and personal growth. But I was not yet fully living from a vibrational place that matched those beliefs and was thus continuing to attract the wrong people.

My brother would tell me, "Your picker is broken." I was determined to repair it. I knew this break was the next right step for me. I had a strong faith and an inner knowing that I would not end up alone forever. But what I did *not* know was how long it would actually take for my "true partner" (how I referred to the man whom I was seeking but did not yet know) to show up. So, I adopted the phrase "patient expectancy." This concept held faith that my partner would come within a time ruled by a force greater than me, even if, in the end, that partner ended up being myself. Regardless of how long it would take, I was clear what needed to happen in the present. I would not seek out dating or any relationship for at least one full year.

A song that touched my heart during that time away from dating was "Let Go of the Shore" by Karen Drucker. She built upon the metaphor of letting go of the safety of the shore and allowing yourself to be carried by a force greater and wiser than you could ever imagine, as if floating on the current of a moving body of water. I envisioned the shore like the bank of a river, and once I released my grasp, I would float downstream in the river current,

61

safely guided, and I could rest. There was no need to continue to struggle, to make any attempts to move upstream, or continue to desperately grasp the shore of what I currently knew and falsely believed that I had some control over.

I loved this simple song as it reminded me to 1) let go, 2) trust that I was being guided and carried, and 3) float into the unknown future, which is a mystery but allowed me to connect with the present, which is all that I need in each moment. During times when I felt deep loneliness, doubted my decision and what would eventually come of it, and yearned for the connection I so deeply desired, these words helped me to remember the same message from "Footprints in the Sand." During my times of trial and suffering, it is then that [God] carries me.

In the meantime, prayer, meditation, journaling, and all the practices I am sharing with you were at the forefront of my experience. Here is an example of one of the spontaneous prayers that emerged from a journal entry while sitting on the beach. This came during an anniversary time, six years post-divorce, when I was struggling financially, parenting an emerging adolescent while also feeling a bit lost and depressed amid this year with myself:

April 3rd, 2016 @ 11:01am ~

Please, God – please, please, please help me to see clearly and receive your grace. Help me to hear your guidance clearly and to follow without distraction. Help me to consolidate where needed and expand where and when necessary. I know these are the ebbs and flows of life, and I know you are here. Please help me to keep going and to strengthen my faith and resolve to endure life's challenges. I release my fear to you, and I surround myself in your love. Thank you for my amazing family, the angels in my life, my friends, my beautiful work, the blue sky, the oceans, the birds, the sand, the breeze, the sun and its warmth, the salt air, and the sound of silence. It soothes me, heals me, and in this very moment, I am okay. I have all that I need, and I am safe and loved, and I am of service using the beautiful gifts you gave to me. Please help me to grow and use those gifts in ways that provide financial sustenance so that my work is supported abundantly. And if I need to tweak it, just keep shining the light in that direction so that I may follow. I will keep moving forward – I promise I won't give up. Thank you, thank you, thank you! Humbly yours – Love, Wendy.

I am confident you will find your own way of speaking with the Divine. Start the conversation and find your own dialogue, your own cadence, and your own relationship. Practice asking. Ask for it all. If you do not ask, you will continue to send blurry messages to the Universe about what you want and need. This vibrational frequency needs to be a clear signal to align you with the life you are deeply yearning for and invite love, joy, peace, and abundance into your experience.

I invite you to connect with prayers from your life thus far that may have spoken to you and write them down, find a copy of them, or otherwise bring them into a space where you can see and read them frequently. Or, as I have demonstrated in this chapter, discover songs that speak the lyrics of your heart and sing them out loud. And then, finally, allow your heart to speak to you in your journal or other creative outlet and express these thoughts, musings, requests, pleadings, struggles, burdens, joys, and sorrows so that you can hear yourself and share these with Spirit. It is always listening, always present, and always there to support you. All you have to do is start the conversation and permit yourself to witness the miracles.

Chapter 6

Meditation—Listen for the Knowing

It was a cold evening in the state of Washington, at a beautiful retreat center in the forest, surrounded by cedar trees and lush flowers. On the property, our teachers had created a path of hot coals and introduced the Firewalk. The exercise aimed to teach a method of getting clear and learning how to listen to and follow your inner knowing. As I walked in a circle around the fiery hot coals with the rest of my cohort, I contemplated, *Will I walk?* I had been given extensive instructions before coming outside to go within myself and allow myself to get *very* clear about whether or not I would walk.

I was in the midst of a two-year internship honing my professional skills in hypnotherapy, breathwork, psychodrama, and transpersonal psychology while also doing deep personal therapy work in the same modalities. We were additionally given many spiritual tools and resources to support ourselves and those we would help with these therapeutic tools.

The firewalk exercise was not about actually walking over the coals. It was about listening to my inner knowing and not succumbing to the pressures of being the only one who doesn't walk, the fear of disappointing my teachers or peers, seeking praise for doing it "right," or proving something to myself or others. This was a very internal exercise and one I took very seriously. I knew in my heart that if I walked for any reason other than my own inner clarity and knowing, I would not get the lesson being provided. I continued to circle the coals.

Intermittently, my peers would come to their own inner decisions and cross the red glowing path. I continued to circle the hot coals. All I kept hearing in my head was, *It's not time.* This message ended up repeating until I trusted that it was not my fear talking or anything but that clear inner knowing. When I'm in a meditative state and hear this inner knowing, I call it "a voice." I often hear it, but you may sense, feel, or even see it.

Even though I was afraid of the coals, I was more afraid of disappointing my teachers. But because this perfectionistic, high-achiever had a history of overriding her instincts and inner knowing to please others, I sensed I had an opportunity here to let go of that old pattern. Deep down, I knew I was working to grow out of that old pattern. I had a deeper sense, a *knowing*, that if I trusted and listened to this inner message, I would discover a part of myself that would never let me down and help me to stop the pattern of self-betrayal that had led to my divorce and other difficult relationships in my history.

So, I listened to and trusted this inner knowing and did not walk across the coals. No one was disappointed. I got the same support and congratulations that everyone else did. I still have the small bag of burned coal and a card from my teachers. The card that is now on my altar reminds me that *I now listen to and follow my inner knowing.*

Funny enough, a few years later, I was back at the same spot, this time as an assistant teacher to another group of students going through the same training I had completed. I was once again facing the firewalk. I had a second opportunity to participate if I wished; this time, I felt called to it. As I walked around the circle this time, it came to me loud and clear: *YES! It's time! GO!* And I walked across the hot coals! With as much clarity as the first time, it reinforced the beauty of listening to and connecting with something much greater than myself that I felt and continue to feel every day.

Meditation is not a way to assume to know what God is thinking or wants you to do. The messages you may receive during your time in meditation are but gentle nudges that invite you to do your own thinking and decision-making. Each message could have an infinite number of interpretations. It is so easy to get caught up in trying to please God when, as I mentioned earlier, if we go with Eckart Tolle's teaching, God has no ego and, therefore, is not attached to whether or not we follow his wisdom.

The firewalk is an extreme example of how I gained clarity, developed a clear sense of my own inner knowing, and learned to understand that higher voice. But not everyone needs a firewalk. There is no one right path to choose. As long as you learn along the way and lean into the connection these tools are helping you cultivate, you will keep moving forward. As a wise friend once told me, "The Universe doesn't have a plan B, so whatever happens is in accordance with your path, no matter what."

Life *is*. There is nothing else you need to do with it except to accept what *is* in each moment, release your resistance to that, and walk forward one step at a time. As another wise friend shared, "You can't move forward by looking backward." Jason Mraz sang about this in his song, "Living in the Moment." He understood that when you focus on the past, you deny yourself the opportunity to fully experience what lies ahead of you on your path. Life only moves forward. Like floating downstream, when you allow yourself to surrender to the present moment and let go of trying to resist the unknown, you will feel more peace, and the very things you dream about or even things beyond your imagination can come into focus. This is what meditation is here to remind you about. You will always find this when you seek to go within, access the present, and listen.

So how do you meditate, you ask? As a beloved teacher once told me, "Just sit down." Honestly, you don't even need to sit. You can meditate standing up, lying down, walking, standing in the grocery store line, or any other place you can take a deep breath and connect with yourself. When you first begin to practice meditation, you may benefit from a more formal and less distractible space. Often, carving out a space in your home or outside in a comfortable nature spot is an excellent place to start. Sitting or lying comfortably with your eyes closed helps you block out the outside world and allows you to go inside.

At first, you may encounter the thoughts and endless chatter that runs through your mind. You might also connect with tension, fluttering, tightness, or other physical sensations in your body. This is all good; it is the beginning. I am often told by those I recommend meditation to that this initial encounter is uncomfortable and why they don't like meditation or believe they can't do it. Discomfort is not something to avoid. It is the precipice of growth. Strengthening your muscles around discomfort allows you to tolerate it better. It gives you more opportunity to discover what lies on the other side of discomfort—often expansion, growth, and new opportunities. I imagine you might be seeking just that! Meditation gives you a way through. It is a practice, a discipline, and will serve you in every aspect of your life.

On the other hand, some folks share that meditation helps them feel connected to themselves for the first time. I would call that coming home to yourself. I hope that coming home to yourself is something that you look forward to and may even be the reason you picked up this book.

The key is to recognize that there is a *you* inside who is observing what may sometimes feel like a committee of conflicting parties all talking at once. Or who may wish to follow these gentle (and sometimes not so gentle) nudges toward something more expansive than your current existence. This inner you can also be referred to as your "higher self," your "authentic self," or your "inner knowing." This part connects to your Source through your unconscious mind and helps deliver the incoming messages to your conscious mind. It is the part of you that is unhindered by your ego's coping mechanisms and conditioned thought patterns and can see a much broader expanse of possibilities than you can often see when you are not connected to it.

When I began to meditate, I experienced an endless chatter in my head and visualized it as ticker tape like the stock prices you see at the top of the screen on a news program. Then, I would lie down as if I could get underneath it and watch it stream above me. Creating some space between me and my thoughts helped me zoom out and gain some perspective on my inner world. I also felt as though I could rest my mind from the incessant thinking always going on.

This is what meditation can afford you. It offers you brief intervals of space from your thinking mind. Taking these periodic breaks from being fused with your thoughts allows you to observe yourself more, thus cultivating a more profound sense of yourself and leading to self-awareness. The more aware you are of your Self, the more choices you have available to you and the less stuck you will feel in situations beyond your control. Giving yourself a break, breathing into the space you've created, and permitting yourself to rest from the doing of life allows you to discover what peace truly feels like and ultimately provides a sense of joy. I humbly subscribe to the belief that joy is not happiness. Joy is more sustainable than happiness. Joy is a state of acceptance and trust in the power and guidance of the Universe.

Meditation is also an excellent way to gain clarity over a situation you are unsure about. This is where prayer and meditation go hand in hand. You may begin your meditation with a question, a concern, a request, something confusing to you, asking for direction or help with a decision. Or, you could start your meditation by stating that you need support and want to be reassured, as Gabrielle Bernstein espoused in her book, *The Universe Has Your Back*. The time spent in meditation is when you get quiet and listen.

Sometimes, I add a card deck to my meditation session to confirm or reinforce the wisdom that comes forth. The card decks I am referring to are not the ones you play poker and bridge with but a deck of cards usually containing pictures and/or inspirational phrases. The cards may be accompanied by a book that explains the deeper meanings behind the cards. Card decks represent many different spiritual traditions. I have a Native American spirit animal deck, an angel card deck, and one called Soulflower, which has various flowers and their meanings. Louise Hay had decks of cards with life-affirming messages on each one. Esther and Jerry Hicks, who write about the law of attraction, have created their own decks. I may even pull out my tarot cards and use the symbols on the cards to provide insight. This list could go on and on.

Before I meditate, I like to pick a deck and spread the cards all out in front of me face down, choose a card I am drawn to, and then use that as an entry into my meditation time. After I complete my meditation, I will allow myself to be drawn to a card and see if that supports what came to me during my meditation. It's a fun addition to your practice that you can experiment with and often amplifies the support you feel when connecting to Spirit in this way.

Having an altar in your home is another tool that helps anchor your meditation space if you wish to have that for yourself. When I began building my altar, it was very simple: a couple of candles, some prayer beads, and some sage or incense. As I grew deeper in my meditation practice, I began to feel called to the altar space with the association that Spirit would meet me there. The symbols I continued to add to the altar assisted me with connecting to myself and the energy of God surrounding me. I now have pictures of my family, some statues that I have collected through the years of Hindu deities, a picture of Jesus from my childhood, a couple of DEMDACO angel statues I received as gifts, candles, sage, sacred rocks from my travels that mean something to me, a singing bowl to call in Spirit with, more prayer beads, and a beautiful tapestry that covers the shelves that comprise the altar's foundation.

I have now dedicated an entire room in my home to house my altar, meditation cushions, a cozy rug, and floor chairs. This is where I come when I need to connect with myself and Spirit and "just sit down." It is also where I feel most inspired and supported to write, which is a very spiritual experience. It is where I feel connected to you, dear reader, and I hope that you can sense the sacredness of our connection as you read the words that flow onto these pages from this space.

Give yourself permission to carve out as much space as you wish to dedicate to your spiritual practice. Everyone deserves a sacred space to connect with Spirit. For you, it may be a corner, a closet, a bookshelf, a space on your patio or in your yard, a particular hiking trail you love, or an entire room just for you. Be creative and follow your heart as you grow and evolve the way you nurture this connection.

Other accessories for meditation might be music and/or a guided meditation where you listen to someone leading you through a visualization or providing prompts to assist you with going inward. Many apps can provide these for you. You can even access some guided meditations on my website should you want to explore more. There are also many types of meditation music. Typically, you would use something without words because lyrics might distract you. Although I have also used songs like the ones described in Chapter 8 to prepare me for a meditation session. I will first play the song and then sit in the silence afterward and allow my mind to quiet down.

One of my favorite types of guided meditation is a *chakra* meditation. Chakra meditations guide you through the seven primary chakras. What is a chakra, you might ask? A chakra is an energy center along your spine from the base to just above your head. Many other chakras are in the body, but the seven primary ones are most often discussed.

Each chakra is associated with a color, a sound, an organ in your body, and certain emotional states. They are visualized as wheels of energy spinning clockwise when opened and counterclockwise when closed. Your goal with chakra meditations is to open these energy centers to help your life force energy flow freely and abundantly, creating more balance and well-being.

You do this by bringing your conscious awareness to each center, allowing each one to open, and releasing anything that you notice no longer serves you or is blocking your energy. Chakra meditations guide you through this process and are wonderful introductions to meditation that you can continue to grow and evolve with as your practice deepens.

Giving yourself the opportunity to listen to and follow your inner knowing is one of the most precious gifts you can give yourself. Meditation is the tool that houses that gift. You don't need a firewalk to connect to it. When you sit down, go within, and listen, you will find it, connect with it, and know it. Once you've made that connection, nothing and no one can take that from you. It is yours to keep, cultivate, and connect with in every moment.

Meditation is a practice that is forever evolving. Allow it to be messy, imperfect, and unique to who you are and wish to become. Enjoy the journey and allow your eyes to open to each and every moment. Notice how meditation gives you a clear vision to see through the illusions that may present themselves

73

to you and carry yourself in a more mindful, conscious way. Feel the balance, grounding, and peace that come with calming your mind and rooting into the present moment. You deserve to have this time with yourself. Just sit down.

Chapter 7

Yoga—Breathe In/Breathe Out

I need to find a way to experience more peace within the chaos of my life.

This reflection came to me as I lay on my yoga mat at the end of a yoga class practicing *savasana*. I would often gain clarity or sense intuitive messages during this time. I was doing this long before I began to meditate more formally, and this was my introduction to what meditation could provide for me. I had become aware that my life was so busy that I was craving space for myself and a way to experience more peace rather than the generalized anxiety and tension I felt in my day-to-day life.

Savasana translates to "corpse pose," which is symbolic of dying in the present moment so that you may be rebirthed into the next. But *savasana* sounds so much prettier and more inviting than the English translation. It is always the last pose in a yoga class. It's a time to integrate your experience during your practice. You lie on your back with your eyes closed, usually listening to beautiful music and your instructor saying things like, "Just rest now. You've done all the hard work. Now, this is time just for you. Let everything else go. There is nothing you need to do or think about at this moment. Allow yourself to integrate all the lessons from your practice and release anything left that no longer serves you."

My awareness came in 2006, while my first marriage was in the beginning stages of deterioration. I was thirty-four years old and felt overwhelmed and pulled in a million different directions. I was providing counseling sessions in my private practice two evenings a month and otherwise committed to being a stay-at-home mom to my toddler at the time. My husband's family was experiencing devastating loss and dealing with that in excruciatingly dysfunctional ways, calling on me to both emotionally and physically attend to them often. My husband had quit his job at a law firm and attempted to start his own business along with a private law practice. He asked me to help with the administrative aspects of the law practice.

We had recently purchased a big house for which we shouldn't have been able to qualify for the mortgage. However, it was 2006 when mortgages were being handed out like candy, and we fell for it. I took on the primary responsibilities for anything the home needed: finances, cleaning, pool care, house repairs, decorating, entertaining family and co-workers, etc. I had a belief, and my husband and in-laws also believed that since I was at home, I had the time and I could do all these things on my own. I was quite convincing in my outward demonstrations that I was capable of anything and always available to help; what other conclusion would they have drawn? I also had no capacity at the time to say no or recognize my limits. I was caring for everybody else in my life, and my needs were on the back burner. I had no idea the toll it was taking on me, but I was beginning to experience the very early signs of burnout.

I taught and practiced yoga for a few years before I became pregnant with my son and also throughout my pregnancy. However, after my son was born, I took a hiatus from yoga and most self-care practices. When he started preschool at two-and-a-half years old, it was a big decision to start yoga again. I sensed a very faint nudge within me to use my son's time in preschool for myself rather than spend every second of my free time attending to the never-ending to-do list and needs of the house and everyone else.

Not having the energy to teach at that time, I found a yoga studio where I could be a student again. I craved a community of like-minded individuals, spiritual connection, and a place to give myself permission to tune in to myself and attempt to make some sense of all the feelings I was experiencing. The studio became my haven. I used to say, "It's the best church I have ever attended." Each time I came to my mat, I felt as though I was having a private meeting with God. I could feel the supportive energy surrounding me when I practiced the postures and relaxed at the end of each class. The more internally quiet I became, the more connected I was to a presence much larger than myself.

Yoga gave me the space I desperately needed and sent me on a path inward to become more aware of my inner landscape. It also anchored me in what it felt like to free myself of my incessant thoughts for a little while. My yoga teachers spoke about the importance of self-care and that I was an important person to consider. Yoga felt safe; it provided me access to a sense of peace and began to point me toward a more compassionate relationship with myself.

When my marriage ended in 2010, my yoga practice gave me the time and space to process and heal the pain, turmoil, and stress of going through a divorce with a young child while trying to build a more solid business. Many times, during a posture or once the practice was over and I was integrating the experience, I would find tears streaming down my face as I had created space in my body for the stored-up emotional energy to finally give way. Yoga can provide a beautiful opportunity to release pent-up emotions or even energy you were unaware of before you came to your mat.

While helping myself heal from the divorce, I gained a new appreciation for the power of "time on the mat." I came to understand that what was happening on the mat reflected what I would experience in my life off the mat. I could take the lessons I was garnering in my practice into my daily life and begin to live more mindfully, more conscious of my body, and more compassionate with my Self.

Simultaneously, I was delving into my advanced clinical training in hypnotherapy, breathwork, psychodrama, and transpersonal psychology and seeking more holistic tools to share with folks in my office. I began to see how yoga could be a natural extension of therapy, and I wanted to understand that connection even more. In 2012, I embarked on a 200-hour yoga teacher training journey to expand my previous certifications and became certified as a Kripalu yoga teacher.

Throughout the years since then, I have spent some time teaching classes and have shared yoga insights and practices with those I work with. Although I no longer teach formal classes at this stage in my life, I continue to practice on my own most days of the week as an extension of my other more intensive weight training workouts. My yoga foundation—both on and off the mat—has provided me with the mobility needed to challenge myself and recover from many types of stressors.

Have you been searching for a way to find peace amidst the chaos or stress in *your* life? Do you crave time for yourself or yearn to feel more connected to yourself? Are you spending more time taking care of others than yourself? Have you ever wondered what yoga was or how to begin? The good news is that yoga is for everybody and is as easy as breathing in and breathing out.

You certainly don't need to attend formal classes at a yoga studio to practice it. However, there is something about being in the energy of a class that provides a safe, supportive space to connect with yourself and with others at the same time. When humans gather in groups, whether it be to worship in a traditional context, to hear each other's struggles in a support or therapy group, to chant devotional songs, or, as in this case, to practice yoga, the energy multiplies and surrounds each person. This powerful experience can exponentially compound your healing and connection to an energy greater than you.

Yet, if classes aren't your thing, yoga is flexible (no pun intended!) and can be practiced anywhere: at home, in your car, at your desk, outside in nature, or in a sacred space you create that calls you to your mat. You don't *need* a mat, although it is helpful to prevent you from slipping all over the place. And some music is a nice accompaniment, although that is up to you. Many of the songs and types of music I will share in Chapter 8 are favorites for my yoga practice. Some people like classical music, some want pop or rock music, and some prefer more inspirational tunes. The bottom line is that you can make your yoga practice whatever you wish. The goal, though, is to have an experience where you tune inward, release the distractions of your life, and get out of your head and into your body. You will find the connection to your spiritual source and an infinite well of creativity and personal power within your body.

Yoga is a moving meditation. So, building on what we discussed in the previous chapter, yoga takes you to another level. Or, you might start with yoga and move into a deeper, more focused meditation practice. They are very complimentary. Yoga postures are a combination of breath, movement, and body awareness. However, yoga is much more than physical postures and cute, trendy outfits. It is a lifestyle that helps you to foster more mindfulness, compassion, and consciousness in all aspects of your life.

Breath, or *pranayama*, is the foundation of yoga. Through your breath, you can connect with a vibrant life force within you that connects you to your Source. In yoga, this energy may be referred to as life force, kundalini, breath of life, or Divine consciousness. It is a direct line to your spiritual connection. The postures, also referred to as *asanas*, are designed to prepare you for meditation. Adding yoga to your routine is a beautiful way to cultivate your spiritual connection and deepen your spiritual practice.

When teaching yoga more regularly, I often reminded people in my classes to "just breathe." This reminder would be repeated frequently throughout the class. I would also suggest that the breath is the most essential part of the practice: "If all you do is sit or lie on your mat and breathe today, you will benefit greatly from this class." I frequently share the teaching that "You cannot breathe deeply and dissociate from your body at the same time." In other words, if you are breathing, you are connected to yourself and your Source. Conscious breathing automatically connects you to your Self, brings you into the present moment, and allows you to move through anxiety, pain, or stress and discover a new experience: presence.

Some folks struggle with the postures. Some may believe that yoga is about forcing your body into pretzel-like positions. Although some postures may seem to invite you to do that, the goal is not to force anything. It is to find acceptance of where you are in the space of that moment and give yourself permission to be wherever you are and move in whatever way your body is capable of in that moment. With consistent continued practice, you will find your way into postures you wouldn't have thought attainable when you first started.

This level of acceptance helps to heal perfectionistic tendencies, self-judgment, and harsh inner critics. Those inner shadows may be who you initially meet on the mat. While in that meeting, you can create more awareness of your thought patterns and old, outdated beliefs about yourself. Then, you will feel more peace by practicing more patience, giving yourself permission to just "be," consciously breathing through discomfort, and allowing your body to relax. Many yoga practices also focus on opening the heart, which will provide space for you to connect with more unconditional love and compassion inside of you that you can share with yourself and those you encounter off the mat.

When I practice yoga at home, I find it fascinating how my cats are drawn to me. Animals seem to pick up on the calming energy yoga creates. It feels safe. When I am in a downward-facing dog position on my mat, my cat will often walk underneath me or lie down at the end of my mat, purring happily. When I relax into savasana, she will curl up next to me and rest. This illuminates how shifting the energy within you affects others around you.

Pets are sensitive to your energy. They respond to what you put out into the world. Humans are equally sensitive, and although many have developed extensive coping mechanisms to hide or protect that vulnerability, it remains nonetheless. Imagine how you might impact your children, your spouse, or even strangers you encounter when you carry this new peaceful energy with you. Just imagine how the cells of your own body will respond to this healthy, peaceful, loving practice you give yourself. In this way, yoga is medicine.

As I alluded to in Chapter 3, yoga is not just about breath and posture. Those are but two of eight limbs of yoga practice as purported by an ancient teacher, Sri Patanjali, who created the foundational yoga teachings called The Yoga Sutras. These teachings existed thousands of years before Christ and have been translated many times. The translation and interpretation from which I share this knowledge with you come from a book provided to me during my Kripalu teacher training entitled *Inside the Yoga Sutras: A Comprehensive Sourcebook for the Study and Practice of Patanjali's Yoga Sutras* by Reverend Jaganath Carrera. It brings the *sutras* into more commonplace language and outlines the foundational principles for a conscious life and what yoga is truly about. To go too deep into this text would be well beyond the scope of this book, but I will attempt to summarize some key principles below for our purposes. Feel free to explore the *sutras* as an additional tool to expand your spiritual connection.

As a lifestyle, yoga is built to pull you out of a state of ignorance and into a state of oneness with the Universe, which may be referred to as a "superconscious state" or "transpersonal" (transcending the ego). Going beyond your limited human mind and utilizing deeper layers of understanding through your actions, your breath, your inner connection with yourself, moving your body to move your energy, your ability to concentrate and focus your energy, quieting your mind, and connecting to a higher consciousness or Spirit.

Practicing yoga through the physical postures connects you to the energy of these teachings. It is the perfect portal to access this pathway of connection to your Source. I encourage you to utilize the infinite collection of videos, books, apps, classes, and instruction our Western world has cultivated over the last sixty years and find what speaks to you. Have fun developing your own practice and begin to witness the shift that occurs with the gifts inherent in this ancient wisdom. As you add this to your garden of resources, you will have easier access to the love, joy, peace, and abundance that come with a quieter, calmer mind and a more flexible body inside and out.

Chapter 8

Music and Mantras—Calling in Spirit

It was January 2010, and I was finally at the hypnotherapy internship I had been dreaming about and struggling to make happen for the past year. I found myself sitting on the floor of a large group room in a retreat center outside Miami, Florida (a satellite location connected to the center in Washington State that I have referenced in earlier chapters). It was 6 a.m., and I had been invited to start my morning with chanting. I had no idea what this was or what this meant, but I was determined to make the most of this experience for myself.

My first husband had moved out of the house a few days before, and we had initiated the process of dismantling our fourteen-year marriage. I desperately needed a safe space to process my feelings around this devastating decision to end my marriage. As I mentioned in the last chapter, yoga was a huge support for me during this time, but I needed even more. I felt utterly lost, burned out, and disconnected from my Self and my spiritual connection. Remember the burnout that began years earlier? Well, by this time, I was charred.

Yes, the chanting. The music started, and I heard the deep sound of an organ (which I later found out is a traditional Indian instrument called a harmonium) coming over the speaker system and filling the room. I felt chills throughout my body. Then, I felt surrounded by a man's voice and his music. I would later learn his name was Krishna Das. The words were sung in the ancient language of *Sanskrit,* so I had no idea what was being said. I simply understood that these words and phrases were names of God or ways to connect to and call upon both masculine and feminine Divine Energy. This greatly appealed to me, and I was excited.

My internship teacher shared with us that chanting was a form of *kirtan,* a call-and-response singing native to Hindu traditions. She had written the lyrics on a large board so we could learn the foreign words, and if we felt inspired, we were encouraged to sing aloud. She had told us to be mindful of feeling the vibration of these powerful words as we allowed them to come out of our mouths and to notice how we felt inside our bodies as we sang.

The purpose of chanting in this context was to call in Spirit to be our guide for the day of teaching, learning, and healing. We were going to be both the therapist and the client in our experience throughout the long weekend together, so not only was I gaining valuable tools and skills I could take back into my counseling practice, but I would also have the opportunity to receive this therapy for my own wounds and broken heart. Our group would also be studying together for the next two years, meeting four times a year, so we were building many ways to bond with our group. Having spiritual support for this sacred work felt amazing and comforting.

Krishna Das sang three songs: *Om Namah Shivaya* (calling in assistance with releasing my ego), *Ma Durga* (calling in the Divine Feminine and the energy of the sacred mother to nurture us), and *Hare Krishna* (a song to call in the Christ Spirit, to honor any discomfort we may be experiencing, and to celebrate the joy of our connection). Once I got past the initial realization that I would not be asked to shave my head and renounce my life to give out flowers and wear brown clothes, I started to feel something. I felt as if I were coming home—home to Spirit, home to myself, home to my heart, and home to safety. The words triggered a vibration deep inside my soul, reverberated through my heart and throat, and emerged from my lips loud and clear.

My first response was to cry. I connected to a deep longing that I'd had for so long that I felt completely lost in my first marriage. I felt as though I was finally calling out to God and being heard. I felt surrounded by a love so consuming that it overwhelmed me, and all I could do was cry. Cry for my broken heart, the little girl in me who had become so consumed with helping, being perfect, and achieving, and my tired and weary Self who had become so lost along the way. The song *Ma Durga* was particularly emotional for me. I felt as if a loving, nurturing, Divine mother was holding me, and it was okay to finally rest. I found myself curling up in my spot on the floor and surrendering to the vibrations of this beautiful song.

By the end of the chanting session, I had fully surrendered and completely connected to Spirit and was full of love, joy, and peace. My face and the area around me were flooded with tears, but I had never felt so relaxed. I felt safe enough to cry and release all I had stored up through the years. It was a beautiful beginning for me, and chanting became a direct conduit to my spiritual connection. I have built upon and expanded this chanting practice through the years, incorporating it into many aspects of my life.

When I meditate or practice yoga, names of different chants will come to me, and I will then seek out and listen to the song. It's funny; understanding the *Sanskrit* words does not matter. It is the vibration they create that matters. The vibration speaks to your subconscious mind, and your soul recognizes these ancient sounds. The message is intuitively felt rather than requiring a literal translation for the mind to figure out.

If you do decide to seek out translations, you will find that chants are prayers and/or consist of a string of names for the Divine. You are calling in that energy by chanting the name of God (in the universal sense). Chants are universal, even though they are rooted in Hinduism and some Sikh traditions, and they are beautiful ways to connect with your Source. *Kirtan* is a wonderful accompaniment to your yoga practice, singing out loud in your car, or even exercising. I went through a phase of using them when I was out for a run or a walk. It made for a fun addition to my morning exercise routine. Chanting has unlimited potential.

Krishna Das was my introduction to chanting, as he is one of the original Westerners who brought chanting to the West directly under instruction from his guru, a North Indian saint named Neem Karoli Baba, aka Maharaj-ji, in the 1970s. However, since then, chanting has spread and expanded and has many different expressions. Exploring the different artists and their interpretations of these beautiful songs can be a fun way of discovering and creating your own chanting practice.

Many modern chants are a combination of both English and Sanskrit words. Some traditional religious hymns have also been used in the context of *kirtan*. One of the most beautiful examples is the rendition of "Ave Maria" by Ashana. It brings to mind the gorgeous acoustics of large cathedrals and always brings tears to my eyes. At the end of this book, I have included an extensive playlist for you as a starting point. My wish is that you find what speaks to you and have fun with your chanting journey.

My chanting practice became a way for me to connect spiritually in my daily life. I then began to see opportunities for incorporating music into my spiritual practice in other ways. I was drawn to other artists outside of the world of chanting who spoke to me spiritually. As I shared earlier, John Denver was my first exposure to music that connected me with the spiritual aspect of nature. After my divorce, I discovered Jason Mraz, Zac Brown, and some Christian artists who spoke of living in the moment, quieting my mind, surrendering, and leaning into the powerful, supportive presence of Spirit. I have also included many of these songs in my recommended playlist. I encourage you to find inspiration in broad contexts. Use music to bring you home to yourself, and remember that you are always loved, supported, and guided.

Mantras are another form of spiritual practice that evolved for me from my yoga teacher training, exposure to chanting, and my love for words. Mantras are words and phrases that come from spiritual texts or are inspired by your own meditation, affirmations that you create for yourself, or even quotes you find online or from favorite books or folks that you admire. You can create a mantra from anything that inspires or helps keep you on track.

Mantras are traditionally used in meditation to help you focus your attention, allowing your thoughts and other distractions to fall away. Some common mantras are: "Om Namah Shivaya," "OM," "Breathe in peace, breathe out stress," or "Thank you." When I meditate, I will often have a phrase come to me that I then turn into my mantra. My mantras have evolved and gone through the different seasons of my life.

Below are a few mantras that were inspired by chants or came to me through meditation. I have listed the full phrase and my interpretation of what it means for me. The *Sanskrit* mantras are also used as chanting songs so that you may find them in different contexts. Feel free to use these or let yourself listen for your own phrases that support and/or motivate you. When you speak these words or listen to them, allow yourself to let the meaning of them come to you rather than trying to pick a meaning and then apply it to your situation.

- *Om Namah Shivaya* – Releasing my ego and embracing humility.
- *Ra Ma Da Sa* – Dancing with God.
- *Om Gam Ganapataye Namaha* – For when I am scared of the unknown or have an obstacle to overcome.
- *Tejase* – Connecting to the ever-presence of God.
- *Ong Namo* – Healing my heart.
- *Aad Guray Nameh* – Embracing a new beginning – feeling surrounded by protection and peace.

- *Hallelujah* – Surrender and acceptance of the unknown or of trying times.
- *I am breathing, I am safe* – For when I need to remember that sometimes breathing is enough.
- *Om Namo Bhagavate Vasudevaya* – To help me know I am never alone.

You might also use an intention as a mantra to help you stay focused on something you would like to manifest in your life. This helps to create an abundance mindset, encouraging you to focus on what you have, what you are grateful for, and what is working rather than what is lacking, not working, or you don't want. For many years, I used the mantra "I have more than enough for all that I need" to help me when I would become afraid that somehow I wouldn't have enough money, energy, time, work, love, or whatever else I feared was lacking in my life. This mantra served to remind me that all my needs are always met and there is more than enough. This helped me to relax and lean on my faith and trust in the cooperative nature of the Universe and that, even when all seems lost, somehow, what I need always shows up at the right time.

Mantras, intentions, affirmations, and positive words have been a foundation for the life I live today. They were building blocks to help me create a vision for the life that I wanted to strive toward after my divorce. Step by step, using the power of these phrases, I created a life that now holds a marriage with a man I had once only dreamed about, a career I had always longed for that is self-sustaining, a well-adjusted, confident, independent, and strong adult son who knows and trusts his own inner knowing, and a balanced, simple, fulfilling way of living that I would have never dared allow myself to wish for before these spiritual tools were implemented.

What do you want to manifest in your life? What do you need support with? What might help you to focus your attention? Give yourself permission to incorporate music, mantras, chanting, and intention into your spiritual practice and witness your life transform into more love, joy, peace, and abundance than you could have ever imagined. Find a theme song to support your journey. Discover your fullest expression and allow your heart to sing!

Chapter 9

Ritual and Ceremony—Anchor Your Connection

I promise I'm not going to ask you to go dancing naked in the forest during a full moon, although if that is what calls to you, then I definitely want you to do that! Ritual often brings up images of mysterious pagan ceremonies; however, ritual exists in all cultures and every spiritual tradition. We also refer to them as ceremonies. Common ceremonies are weddings, funerals, graduations, confirmations, engagements, coming-of-age celebrations, birthdays, anniversaries, communion, baptism, pilgrimage, etc. They often signify the beginning or end of something and are a way to mark the chapters of our lives. But there are infinite opportunities to create your own personal rituals to anchor your spiritual connection or anchor the beginning or end of something significant to you in your life.

Rituals are honestly my absolute favorite tool in this book. I have participated in many formal rituals to mark important times in my life, but I was also drawn to create my own as more personal milestones emerged along my journey. It seems fitting to share the stories around the personal rituals I have created rather than talk about them. There are three primary stories I would like to share, although many small rituals occur in my day-to-day life that might better be referred to as "daily practice."

Out of rituals and ceremonies emerge symbols, wisdom, expansion, growth, and typically some type of release of something that no longer serves you and a receiving of something new to carry. Think about times in your life when you may have experienced something like this but didn't perceive it or refer to it as a ritual. I'm sure you have your own stories. As you read through the rest of this chapter, you may begin to understand how you can integrate ritual into your own spiritual practice to continue enhancing your spiritual connection.

Rituals can be powerful invitations for Spirit to join you in your experience. They are also a way to deeply anchor your intentions. Rituals are sacred and provide a beautiful way to strengthen your connection to spirit and witness the support and abundance that can emerge as a result.

The Vision Quest:

In addition to the firewalk, I was offered an opportunity to experience a powerful Native American ritual called a vision quest. The traditional use of this ceremony is to assist you with connecting to Spirit and "calling for a vision." In other words, you ask Spirit for clarity, direction, and an understanding of your life path or to reveal the next right step. My vision quest was hosted by a Native American tribe on land located on the outskirts of Sedona, Arizona. I went with a group of fellow students and had a life-transforming experience.

I was drawn to the vision quest as an opportunity to get as close to God as possible. I was also turning forty a week before it was scheduled, and I thought this would be a perfect way to transition into midlife and mark this special birthday. I was informed that this would be a four-day and night experience where I would be "placed" out on a marked spot on the land by myself and picked up on the fifth morning. There were to be no worldly distractions. I was allowed to bring a tarp, a sheet, a sleeping bag, a few layers of clothing, a spade, and the prayer ties I had made during my preparation period. That was it—no food or water for *four* twenty-four-hour periods. No journal. No music. Nothing but me, the natural surroundings, and God.

We began to prepare for this experience one year ahead. I spent that year studying more about this Native American ritual, recognizing how blessed I was as a non-Native to experience this sacred ceremony, and going deep within to connect with Spirit and pray. This is where prayer ties came in. Prayer ties serve a few different purposes. They are made of red 2x2 cloth squares, rope twine, tobacco, blessings, and prayers. For one entire year, in several sittings, I created 365 individual prayer ties strung in succession. For each cloth square, I would place a pinch of tobacco and waft sage over it as I added my prayer. My prayers asked Spirit for protection, for help with releasing fears, requests to watch over my fellow questers, for keeping my son safe while I was gone, for calming my son's anxiety about me leaving, for my family, for my friends, for anyone else who needed prayers, for gratitude for the experience, for a clear vision, for anything else that I carried on my heart at the time. I would then create a tiny bundle out of the cloth and secure it to the twine strand. The strand was wrapped around a cardboard square with slats cut into the edges so that it would not become entangled. This was an incredibly powerful exercise, and that was all before I even arrived in Sedona.

As the year unfolded, I felt more and more prepared and less and less scared. My heart was wide open, and I was actually quite vulnerable energetically, which was good for the vision quest but sometimes tough as I continued to interact with the outside world during those months of preparation.

I was very cautious about who I told about this journey I was embarking on and saved all the details for those in my closest inner circle. I learned this the hard way. Initially excited about signing up for the quest, I told an acquaintance what I was doing. She freaked out and promptly told me that I would not survive without water for four days, that I was being an irresponsible parent for putting myself in this position with a young son, and that they thought I had absolutely lost my mind. Yet I felt this was one of the sanest decisions I had ever made, and I trusted the process and the Universe enough to know I would be safe. Nevertheless, I learned that not everyone would be able to digest this kind of adventure.

In October 2012, I flew to Arizona and joined the other "questers." We all converged upon this Native land and spent the first night in tents and when we couldn't sleep, around a campfire. We learned that this fire was a sacred part of the ceremony and would be tended to for the entire time we would be out in our spots by "supporters," who would remain by the fire and pray for us during those four days.

At sunrise the next morning, a medicine man greeted us, led us through a sacred ceremony, and provided each of us with a sacred blessing. Usually, he was adorned in traditional garments, including the most gorgeous headdress made of eagle feathers.

He then led us out in order to be placed in our spots. I witnessed each person being guided to their spot, placed inside a small square of land marked by four stakes (to signify the four directions) that were tied off with our prayer ties. The prayer ties would serve as a boundary and protection, marking our spot. Then, we would travel to the next person's spot and so on until we got to my spot.

I was placed under a juniper tree with a view of distant rolling hills out in front of me, and to my left was a large formation of red rocks that typically represent the Sedona landscape. A small space had been cleared of all brush and sticks and rocks. This was my spot. It was made lovingly by the hands of the supporters just for me. I felt loved by this gesture. I also felt safe knowing folks would be praying for me, and I was committed to the process, even though I had no idea exactly how I would survive all of this. But I had faith, a willingness to trust, and a clear knowing that this was a step I needed to take.

As I watched the other questers fade out as they traveled toward the next person's spot, which was out of my sight and earshot, the sounds quieted down. I took stock of my surroundings and laid out my tarp and sleeping bag. It had been quite chilly the night before but was warming up to be very pleasant. The sun was shining, the sky was blue, and the scenery was spectacular. Then I settled in. I tend to enjoy time with myself in solitude, so that was greatly welcomed. However, I had never slept out in the elements before, and I was afraid that an animal or insect would try to crawl into my sleeping bag during that first night.

As the sun descended behind me in the west, I realized I was facing east. I would have a direct view of the sunrise each morning. That came to be my saving grace. I slept a couple of hours that first night and woke up to a completely clear sky full of stars. There was no electricity for miles and no moon, so every star was visible and illuminated above me. I could see the Little Dipper, the Big Dipper, and several other constellations. But I came to understand that an hour or so before the sky showed its first light, the Big Dipper was completely visible as it rose over the rock formation on my left. Over the next few nights, when I would wake up and wonder how much longer it would be dark, I would look for the Big Dipper, and that would reassure me that the best movie I have ever seen would soon begin.

As it got close to sunrise, I would sit up, still wrapped in my sleeping bag, and assess my situation. The first morning, I had some frost on my sleeping bag, which made for some moisture to rub on my face and lips. I was still breathing, had saliva, and felt pretty good. I was completely enthralled when I watched the sunrise over the mountains in the distance. I have no idea how many hours I sat like that, but I felt total peace and gratitude for the sun, the light, the morning, and the ability to appreciate it all. By the end of the second day, I was feeling a bit nauseous and unsure whether I would make it through the whole four days. Would I actually be able to do this? I told myself that I would stay through the second night, and if I woke up feeling the same way, I would consider trying to find my way back to the supporters' camp.

But to my surprise, wonder, and humble awe, I felt great the next morning! It was as if my body had shifted into a mode that could function without food and water. I had total mental clarity and felt as though I was buzzing on the inside with energy. Physically, I was tired and could not move around much, but I felt very alive. And I was so proud of myself for not giving up. I came to trust in the power of this process even more, and all my fears were gone. All the prayers I had filled my prayer ties with surrounded me, and all the prayers that the supporters and others back home were sending our way provided comfort. I felt loved and held and safe and free.

On the fifth morning, I awakened to my new best friend, the Big Dipper, and I sat up for my new love, the sunrise. I realized I still had saliva in my mouth, although it had been almost ninety-six hours since my last drink of water. I was alive. I said to myself aloud, "I am still here!" And I woke up with the deepest knowing that *I am here by the Grace of God and the Power of Prayer.* Although I had many inspirations and ideas throughout my time on the Quest, I knew this was the vision I had been seeking. To fully surrender and trust in my relationship with Spirit and to know that my communication with my Source is powerful and reciprocal was the gift that this experience brought from deep in my soul into my conscious awareness. I knew that the lessons from this experience would be ongoing, and this was a beginning for me on a path to unlimited possibilities. I was excited to begin a new leg of my journey. I also knew that I was forever changed and transformed and would never approach my life quite the same again.

When Uqualla and the supporters came to get me on that fifth morning, immediately after sunrise, I was relieved to see them but also timid to return to the earthly world of other humans, distractions, responsibilities, and noise. It took me a couple of weeks to fully reintegrate into my life, and I felt very protective and private about my experience for several months afterward. I realized this was so personal and deep for me that sharing it seemed to minimize it somehow because others who had not experienced it had no way of understanding. But I didn't need others to understand. This was between me and God. And that relationship has only grown deeper in the years since that time under the Juniper tree.

Below is a journal entry I wrote on the plane home from Sedona about twenty-four hours after leaving my sacred spot.

Thursday October 18, 2012 @ 10:40 am:

On my way home from Vision Quest. Just spent the last four days in Sedona, AZ, in a beautiful space and challenged myself beyond all my expectations. I did it!! I was surrounded in love, and I believe the whole process was a miracle. The love and support I felt was tremendous and carried me through. My most profound insight was gratitude and complete humbleness at the power of God's grace and the power of prayer. It is by these two things that this was possible. They gave me the strength to endure no food or water, elements, animals, peeing and pooping outside, sitting alone in a small space, sleeping alone outside in the dark, with absolutely no distractions from the outside world. I tuned into nature, the sunrise and sunset, the stars, the wind, the sounds of the animals, and the pure silence. It was awesome and challenging all at once. So many ideas and insights and pure knowing came to me. It will take me months to incorporate, but I know that it changed my life for the better. My mind expanded and cleared and connected to that Great Spirit that is so much greater than me but in and through which I can do great things to bring a bit more love and consciousness to the world.

The lessons: I am FREE. If something is promised to you, it cannot be lost or taken away. It stays as long as it needs to, and when it goes, it's time, and we let go. This is my new insight now for relationships going forward. I have no need to control things. Just enjoy each moment and stay connected to my heart. Patience and present-moment awareness are key.

The Ant: Patience. The Fly: Persistence: We don't need to be omnipresent with those we love. Love is the sustaining force—no need to try and hold on tight and communicate incessantly. Just let it be, and when the time comes to have time together, enjoy it and stay true to my heart and truth. Really can relax around that. Less is more.

They say that the four days following a quest are an extension of it—so I'm still in it. I feel as though I am operating at a higher vibration and very vulnerable. Just very conscious of taking care of myself and loving me back into the world, just as though I was a newborn baby. Oh, there is so much to write! But I will take it in steps. I need to rest now.

I love you so much Wend! I'm SO proud of you! You are SO strong and beautiful. You did it! Let it sink in and enjoy!!

Sharing my story of the vision quest from the vantage point of ten years later has helped me gain perspective on the direction I was steered in from that moment forward. It didn't immediately clear up all the dysfunction in my life. However, it *did* set me on a path to completely transform my business and eventually get a lot clearer about my relationship direction, and it affected how I see the world, parent, and interact with Spirit. It even prepared me to share this book with you today. That is a true miracle.

Putting Out the Call for a Partner:

In the seven years after my divorce, I spent a lot of time with myself. I experimented with online dating and had a couple of significant long-distance, long-term relationships. Yet, I continued to struggle with what felt like unfinished business from my past relationship patterns. This irony was not lost on me as a marriage and family therapist. What I appreciate about my profession is that it offers me room to learn about and explore aspects of myself that would not otherwise be in my awareness. I believe that my responsibility as a therapist is to do my own personal work and be willing to be vulnerable and open to learning so that I can better help others to do the same. I subscribe to the idea that "We teach what we most need to learn."

In light of this awareness, in the summer of 2015, as I referred to in an earlier chapter, I made a conscious decision to take a year off from dating and relationships and be in a relationship with myself. This seemed like a radical notion for a person who has always been laser-focused on relationships, and at first, I wasn't even sure if I could do it. However, as the year went on, I began to understand the benefits of this conscious time with myself and got to know myself on a very deep level. Over time, I came to honor and revere my commitment and became unwilling to dishonor myself in any way.

When the year concluded, I felt it appropriate to mark this time with a sacred ceremony and happened to have a perfect place and opportunity to create this out in Washington during a training weekend with my fellow students. Drawing on my vision quest experience, I chose to use prayer ties and the sacredness of fire to consecrate this life chapter. In addition to marking the end of my year with myself, I intended to consciously "put out the call" for a healthy relationship to enter my life.

I spent several months once again making 365 prayer ties to mark each day of what became a sacred time with my Higher Self. I built upon the relationship with Spirit that I had expanded during my vision quest, which was once again expanding. I had created even more space for God to connect with and guide me and for me to lean in and trust in the power of my intuition. I like to think of intuition as the nudge of Spirit from within.

I wanted to write something special to read at the ceremony describing what I connected to and discovered during this year. I sat with these thoughts for several weeks leading up to my journey out to Washington, and while flying across the country, the words came to me. I could also envision the entire ceremony. Each training weekend would close with a sweat lodge. A fire was built to heat the rocks for the sweat lodge, and we would all gather around the fire before entering the lodge. My idea was to use that time around the fire to read my words and then toss the prayer ties into the fire to officially put out my call and humbly offer my prayers and requests to Spirit. My cohort, whom I had come to know and love as my spiritual family, would bear witness to this. With ritual and ceremony, we often invite friends and loved ones to witness. Witnesses tend to enhance the energy of what is being celebrated or consecrated but are not always necessary. For this particular event, though, I thought it pertinent.

This felt so big to me. I knew deep in my soul that to change my vibrational frequency from the dysfunctional codependent patterns I had been locked in thus far, I needed something drastic. Well, this was pretty drastic. I see now that the vision quest was the beginning of this shift. And this was my next step.

Below are the words that describe my intimate reflection on this year with myself. It seems fitting to include in this chapter on ritual, as it was one of the most powerful rituals of my life to date. It may inspire you to create your own ritual to mark a sacred time in your life. Or maybe you will find something in it that soothes you, inspires you, or puts words to your own yearnings or experiences in some way.

The Year I Fell in Love with Myself

Wendy Elizabeth Crane – July 1, 2015 – June 30, 2016

Read during my Prayer Tie Ceremony on July 10th, 2016

I was struggling, drowning, in the unconscious, addictive, and dysfunctional patterns of my past.

As I breached the surface, I noticed a hand reaching out to me.

I grabbed it and was finally able to catch my breath.

She offered me respite from the chaos.

She asked me to rest upon the shore with her for one year.

I automatically agreed - not a decision of my mind but from deep within my soul—

A knowing that the survival and redemption of my heart depended on it.

During that year on the shore, I cycled, I learned, I trusted, I cried, and I celebrated.

I risked and I hid.

I lamented and I sighed deep relief.

I rested and I dreamed.

I released shame, fear, hurt, and anger.

I relentlessly maintained this commitment.

I came to understand what it meant to truly love and care for another and what that kind of love truly felt like to receive.

I settled down and settled in as it became very clear to me that the hand who had reached out for me in the treacherous waters was my own.

I made peace with myself.

I fell in love.

This recognition and cultivation of deep connection filled in the gaps of my being.

It has been a blissful reunion, as though I have been gone from myself for centuries.

As I re-pixelated, I excavated and honed and strengthened my wild instincts, my human earthly cycles, and came to trust in my intuition and intimate connection to the Divine Energy of Life Force that I consist of. This Life Force completely inhabits and surrounds me and merges with everything else in the Universe.

From this perspective and experience of Divine Union, I humbly put out the call for a special man to come and join me on this journey.

I call to Grace as the messenger, and I invite her to unite us with a deep knowing of each other as if we have been here all along together.

I know that possibilities are infinite when the Grace of God and the Power of Prayer merge.

So, I now lift up my humble and sincere prayers to Spirit so that prayer and grace may head my call. I am ready.

With earnestness, patience, trust, and humility, I stand before you. My heart is open.

105

I revere and hold sacred this time spent on the shore.

I am forever grateful for the lessons of love I have learned. They are deeply anchored.

My greatest gift is the love I have created for and with myself. This gift is mine to continue to cultivate. I now have so much more to share with an intimate partner.

I pray to share and honor my love with a man who is willing and able to love me from an equally secure and sacred and loved place within himself.

I go forth with a spirit of enthusiasm, excitement, and expectancy. My heart is overflowing . . .

AHO!

I'd love to be able to tell you that I flew home and met the man of my dreams the following week. But alas, Spirit tends to have different timing than humans here on Earth. However, I maintained my faith and the clear commitment that I would never again settle for any person or relationship that was less than what I wanted and deserved. I was worth it and unquestionably trusted in the cooperative nature of the Universe. My job was to stay true to myself, release any form of self-betrayal, and harness "patient expectancy." I was absolutely sure in my bones that I was not meant to spend this entire lifetime by myself, but I had no idea when this partner of mine would show up. As the months passed, I even allowed myself to accept that this "partner" may be me. I rather liked myself as a relationship partner at that point, so I was willing to stay open to that option. In the meantime, I lived my life on my own terms.

Building a Conscious Relationship from the Inside Out:

I guess the Universe had its own plans for me. Exactly nine months later (funny how it seems that my "call" incubated for the same amount of time it takes for a new life to form in the womb), I sensed this gentle nudge to try online dating. I vehemently opposed this for a long time, but something was calling me. I was very clear that I would not return to the mainstream dating sites, but I wanted to try out a site that was more spiritually focused, as I had also become very clear that the most important thing to me in a new relationship would be the ability to connect on a spiritual level. So, I found a site focused on connecting more spiritually inclined singles, and I made a profile. I had decided to dip my toe in the water, not pay for a full membership yet, and just look at who was on there.

As I suspected, my selection was very slim, including international men in different countries, men much older than me, and many who did not warrant my time. However, there was this *one* guy. I reached out, we emailed for a couple of weeks, and I eventually went on a date with this man who later became my current husband, David. As we got to know each other over those first weeks and months, I began to recognize the man in front of me was exactly who I had asked for during my prayer tie ceremony. During that year on my own, I had also curated a fairly extensive description of *the man I love* to describe this partner who I dreamed of having and trusted would come. Yet I also secretly wondered if my request was a bit much, even for the most powerful energy. Well, you will never know what is possible if you don't at least ask, right? I took out this descriptive list a couple of months into our relationship, and I realized that I had described David to a complete tee! He was everything on my list and more. He literally was the man beyond what even my imagination could conjure up.

This furthered my trust in the power of ritual and how connecting to your Source can help create a life aligned with all that you wish for and more. When you do the work and use the tools available to you to cultivate this powerful connection, anything is possible. And the promises of love, joy, peace, and abundance become part of what feels like the natural flow of your life.

What is it that your heart is calling for? What would you like to honor through ceremony? You can ask for support and guidance from the Universal Spirit, which is so much more creative, powerful, and resourceful than you are alone and can manifest miracles in any and all ways.

As I was getting the hang of these rituals, I wanted to incorporate this practice into my relationship with David. I was coming to see him as my true life partner—the man I was meant to be with for the remainder of my time here on Earth. One of the many things that made David my true partner was that he thought these types of practices were important and valuable, too.

We sought out books to help us learn more about what a "conscious relationship" consists of. As we began to read the books *Conscious Loving* and *The Conscious Heart* by Gay and Kathlyn Hendricks, I saw another opportunity for us to contribute to the foundation of our relationship through ceremony. I was determined not to repeat the patterns of my past and to bring in the knowledge I had gained from the vision quest, from the year with myself, and my prayer ties ceremony. I wanted a conscious relationship and nothing less.

From *The Conscious Heart,* I borrowed what the Hendricks' refer to as The Six Co-Commitments along with their foundational relationship statement entitled "The Master Commitment." I typed them up and laminated a 4x6 copy for both David and me to have as reminders of the foundation and framework we were working to create together, as he had the same dream of building a conscious relationship (but that story is for another book). I requested that we go down to the lake near David's house and read these commitments out loud to each other. He agreed. It was our own private commitment ceremony. We each read aloud *The Master* Commitment and The Six Co-Commitments. Then, we each hung the laminated cards where we could read them each day and referred to them often as we worked to stay true to what we had committed to that day at the lake.

A couple of years later, we created a more formal ceremony that we are all familiar with when we married in front of our closest friends and family. Weddings are traditional ceremonies and often have a formal script that they follow. However, we wanted our wedding to be a personal reflection of the conscious relationship we had diligently built together and to include these commitments we had come to use as a framework for a healthy relationship. We had read more books by then: *Passionate Marriage* by David Schnarch and *The Seven Principles for Making Marriage Work* by John Gottman and Nan Silver. These books became the foundation for our new marriage and our way out of old codependent, dysfunctional, unconscious relationships that had led to our previous struggles and breakups.

As we got closer to our wedding date, we were naturally dealing with the stresses of planning a wedding and entering into this formal commitment that we knew in our bones was right but nevertheless can trigger some anxiety. I had decided to utilize one of my spiritual tools to help keep me grounded and give me a place to stay connected to myself and the Source that brought us together and to this moment.

> *Thursday, April 25, 2019 @ 8:43 am – Two Days Before Our Wedding:*
>
> *Reading Eckhart Tolle this morning—he defined Ananda as "the bliss of being." That is my spiritual path, and finding David as my partner to walk with who wants to focus on be-ing is so divinely inspired, guided, and right. When I stay rooted in being, I feel peaceful, alert, and full of love and appreciation. When my thinking takes over, I end up with a do-ing overload. So, striking a balance is most important and giving myself the gift of being every day is part of that, so I never lose touch with it.*
>
> *As I watch the baby ducks waddle across my yard in front of my porch, I feel joy. As I listen to the stillness behind the day-to-day sounds, I feel peace. I am so grateful for this awareness in this experience. And today begins our long weekend of celebration. It anchors the love between David and me in ritual and consciousness. All of our witnesses begin their journeys to us over the next couple of days, and most of us will come together tomorrow evening for a pre-wedding dinner. Then Saturday is our official celebration! My intention is to walk through each moment with a present awareness and allow myself to soak it all in. I am so proud of David and me for putting this all together and for creating something so meaningful and beautiful.*

Thank you, God and all the angels and benevolent forces of the Universe, for all of your support, guidance, and magical influence as we have walked along our path to this place, and I know you will continue to walk forward with us into each moment from here.

Wendy - this has been quite a life so far, and there is so much more to create as you ride out this earthly journey. But the most important experience is right now, and I celebrate the work you have done thus far to be able to even know that so clearly. You're absolutely beautiful and precious and full of love. Allow your heart to open, let all fear be released, and shine your light out for all to see, and love, love, love!

I love you so much! Enjoy every single moment!

Love, Ananda

Friday, April 26th, 2019 @ 8:30 am – One Day to the Wedding!

Our wedding is tomorrow! It's hard to believe it's finally here! Feeling a vibration of excitement within me. That is the undercurrent of my experience today. The weather is shaping up beautifully as all of our guests begin to converge on the Orlando area today. All of our planning and preparation on all levels is coming to fruition, and tomorrow I get to marry a man who, at one time, was only a figment of my imagination.

Thank you, God, all the angels and benevolent forces of the Universe, for the beautiful gift of David and for exceeding my vision well beyond what I could dream up by myself. I cherish the sacredness of these next two days and carry that forward for every day thereafter.

Thank you, thank you, thank you!

These journal entries reflect the power of the tools I'm sharing with you. Through the years, from my divorce until my second marriage, I cultivated a deep spiritual connection. I journaled my way back to myself, moved my body with yoga, conversed with Spirit through meditation and prayer, and filled my mind and heart with the lyrics of inspirational music and mantras. I sat in nature, and I participated in ritual. It all culminated in this moment, where I once again walked down an aisle, but this time fully conscious, fully connected to my true Self, and fully clear that I was here for all the right reasons to connect with a man brought to me by my most entrusted Source. I was fully committed and ready to voice just what I was committing myself to in front of God and our witnesses.

We incorporated the commitments from our early readings right into our wedding ceremony. Below are our vows, adapted and expanded from the books *Conscious Loving* and *The Conscious Heart* by Gay and Kathlyn Hendricks.

The Master Commitment

I accept relationship itself as my primary teacher about myself, other people, and the mysteries of the Universe. I open myself to letting every relationship interaction, no matter how seemingly trivial, deepen my connection with my essence and the essence of others. I invite all healing powers in myself and the Universe to remove any obstacles to my relationships, being a source of joyful fulfillment to me in all my depths.

I make a commitment to intimacy that is greater than my commitment to being right and perpetuating my conditioned patterns.

112

Our Commitments to Each Other

I commit to being close and to clearing up anything in the way of doing so. I also commit to honoring my essence rhythms of both closeness and separateness and to learning about and honoring your essence rhythms as you come to understand them.

I commit to my own complete development as an individual, to learning to love and appreciate myself and my essence. I commit to expanding into the fullest expression of my own creativity.

I commit to the full empowerment of you, my partner, to learning to love and appreciate you at the deepest level and honoring and inspiring your full creative expression.

I commit to taking full, healthy responsibility in our relationship, including my happiness, my well-being, and my life goals. When faced with the choice of being happy or being defensive, I commit to choosing happiness.

I commit to revealing rather than concealing, to holding back nothing and telling the unarguable truth about everything. I also commit to listening nonjudgmentally to what you share with me.

I commit to having a good time in our relationship, to celebrating life with you, and to play, laugh, and have fun together as we navigate whatever the universe has in store for us to experience.

The Rings

I give you this ring as a symbol of my commitment to you and to our family and of the beautiful love and life we create one step and one day at a time together.

We continue to refer to these commitments in our day-to-day interactions, and each year, on our anniversary, we re-read them to each other. They have helped to keep us on track to remember that we were brought together to learn and grow, that marriage is not always rainbows and butterflies, but it is solid and holds the capacity for each of us to expand into our best and highest selves. We know without a doubt that we are supported by Spirit, and whenever we get lost or feel off-center, we pick up our tools, and we always, always, always find our way back.

Give yourself a chance to harness the power of ritual to call in, strengthen, mark, honor, and celebrate the things you deem important in your life. As you might take a picture to capture a moment in time or recall the importance of something, ritual and ceremony can further anchor your experience and coordinate with Spirit to support you in what you wish to mark as sacred. The possibilities are limitless. When you utilize all the tools available to you and align with your spiritual connection, the direction of your life can unfold into something beyond your wildest dreams. The promises of love, joy, peace, and abundance move beyond promises into your everyday experience.

Chapter 10

Nature—Spirit Is Everywhere and In Everything

Nature as a conduit and tool for cultivating your spiritual connection brings us full circle back to that poster my father gave me at five years old and his inscription on the back. Nature is the simplest way to connect with Spirit, as all it takes is for you to step outside or look out a window. Just allow yourself to breathe in the fresh air and to notice the colors, shapes, and textures of your surroundings. Use all your senses to take in the sound of the birds, the shape of the trees, the colors and smells of the flowers, the grass, the sand, the water, the mountains, and whatever constitutes the scenic backdrop of your life.

As my father noticed in me at a very early age, I was always drawn to natural elements and curious about nature. I liked studying leaves and flowers and taking in huge gulps of fresh air anytime I was outside. I noticed how the different seasons smelled, and I was tuned into the shifts in temperature and the rhythms of the seasons. I felt very at home climbing trees, lying in a meadow, or hiking in the mountains. As I mentioned earlier, skiing was a large part of my growing up, and getting to the top of that mountain was how I got to God as far as I was concerned.

When I am outside, I feel less constrained by the barriers of walls and ceilings and compartments that seem to disconnect me from Spirit. Although I have many ways of connecting to Spirit that occur indoors, I feel the least inhibited connection when outside. Whenever any of the other tools are practiced outside, it only enhances the experience.

What is your favorite outdoor landscape? Do you prefer the mountains, the forest, the beach, lakes, a city park, or a country back road? What draws you there? What do you like most about your favorite place? If you are not outside while reading this, allow yourself to close your eyes for a moment and visualize your favorite scenery and what it feels like to be there. Notice yourself feeling a bit more present. Or if you are near a window or happen to be reading outside, take stock of your surroundings, connect with something within your range of vision, and focus on it for a moment. Notice what you feel.

I tend to feel more present and sense the aliveness of whatever I am looking at. Everything in nature is alive and, in my mind, is an extension of Spirit. Once again, as Shug Avery in *The Color Purple* shared, "My first step from [the vision of God as an old white man with a beard] was trees. Then air. Then birds. Then other people. But one day, when I was sitting quietly and feeling like a motherless child, which I was, it came to me: that feeling of being a part of everything, not separate at all. You ever notice that trees do everything to git attention we do, except walk?"

This is how I felt on top of the peaks in Breckenridge. The mountains were alive, and I could feel the energy radiating through the chilly winter air and the snow on my bottom when I would sit and stare at the never-ending view. Sometimes, it was so profound that I would sit and cry, feeling the longing of being so close yet somehow not fully able to connect. I have spent the remainder of my adult life seeking to strengthen that connection. And nature is like an instant hookup.

○

My grandfather died in 1980. I was seven years old. Within the next two years, it became apparent that my grandmother would need to sell the beautiful home in the Maine countryside she and my grandfather had built and retired in. She eventually sold it to a family named "The Towners," as we always referred to them. The Towners attended the same church as my grandmother and became fast friends. One day, Mrs. Towner told my grandmother about a camp nearby that her family owned on Great Moose Lake. A camp is a New England term for what most would call a small cottage-style home on a lake. Mrs. Towner invited my grandmother to use this camp anytime and bring her family along.

That following summer, I was about ten years old when she brought my family and my mother's brother's family out to enjoy a week at the camp. On our first visit, this structure was extremely primitive: no hot water, no shower, very basic accommodations, a full kitchen, running water pulled in from the lake, a cozy interior of knotty pine walls and cabinets, and very lived-in furniture. My brother and I and our cousins slept in a loft upstairs with exposed wooden beams, and as far as we were concerned, we were in Heaven! We had no television, phone, or distractions—merely a lake and some floats, a small fishing boat, and time without a schedule.

We affectionately referred to this place as The Yellow Camp because, as you might imagine, it was painted yellow. We began to visit every summer thereafter. The yellow camp became a sacred and revered place for my family. We all felt the magic that seemed to happen when we arrived there. As we stepped out of our car, after driving fifteen hours from Northern Virginia in our family station wagon, I would first run out to the lake and step up on this giant rock that marked the shoreline. I would be hit in the face by the silence. Even as a young tween and into my teenage years, this was profound to me and extremely comforting. I knew that whatever had been happening in my life up to that point would be washed away, transmuted, transformed, and healed by the lake.

The lake truly is the star of the show here. From the camp shore, we have a broad view of a large lake that sparkles in the sunlight and moves with the direction of the wind current. Families of loons occupy it in the summertime; at night, you can hear them calling each other with the most beautiful sound. It is both haunting and inviting at the same time. Loons seem magical in their appearance and in the fact that they are elusive. They dive underwater to feed on fish and pop up to the surface for brief moments. As a family, we have come to feel a blessing of sorts if a loon pops up near the shore, the boat we are floating in, or better yet, alongside the kayak we are paddling.

The lake is always cold. But in those early years, when there was no shower and less global warming, my grandmother would round everyone up in the mornings and announce in a sweet yet authoritarian way that only she possessed, "We need to begin our day with a swim in the lake!" It was freezing, but we willingly participated because we loved her and her enthusiasm for this morning ritual.

As the years went on, this spot became more and more beloved to our family, so when Mrs. Towner eventually informed us that she would be putting the camp up for sale, my parents happened to have come into the funds to be able to purchase it. The timing was perfect, and I will give myself permission to believe it was all divinely orchestrated. We could now officially call this place ours. That was in 1994. We had been happily going to the camp for years, but now had some flexibility to make a few upgrades— like a shower and hot water for starters!

Since then, my parents have made the camp more livable and comfortable but still retain the cozy character of the original. We also now own the house next door and affectionately refer to that as The Red Camp as, you guessed it, it is red. And the lake has continued to provide sacred experiences for the next generation of my and my brother's kids.

These days, the lake is a sanctuary for me. Looking out at the view or being out on the water uninhibited is my closest experience to Spirit. Now that I reside in Florida, skiing is not as much in my everyday wheelhouse. Let's face it: winter is not as appealing to me after being in the sun and warmth all year round. But the lake calls to me more at this stage in my life.

In 2020, during the first summer of the coronavirus pandemic, my husband and I were fortunate to get to Maine by ourselves for a whole week. Once we navigated a masked plane ride and a trip to the local Walmart, essentially, we quarantined at The Yellow Camp for that week. While lying out on the dock, connecting with the lake during all of that uncertainty and fear about what was happening to our world, the following journal entry was inspired and captured my sacred relationship with this spiritual place.

Thursday July 20th, 2020 @ 1:45pm:

Sitting out on the dock soaking in the magical healing Spirit of the lake. It's quiet, with a couple of folks off in the background and a couple of loons echoing in the distance. Otherwise, it's just the lake and the birds and the amazing silence. David and I have been here for three days, and so far, it's been exactly what we both needed. I've had some very special moments with the lake as I've given myself permission to truly tune into my own differentiated rhythm and just follow my own instincts to meet my own needs as I also stay connected to, but not fused, with David. What an amazing gift to give myself! So, along the way, here are some musings that have crossed my mind (maybe for a book someday!):

The Healing Lake

The lake is a living being.

It gives you whatever you are needing and it always knows.

Its breezes cleanse and heal.

It follows the direction of the wind and it never questions.

It asks nothing of you, yet it calls you into your Self, just by the peace and silence it emanates.

Thus, in the end, you surrender and discover the amazing gift of Being in its presence.

When I sit out in the water, on the edge of the dock or in the kayak, as though I am a part of it, and it of me, I feel love and loved.

I realized I am in love with the lake. It's been a love affair I have stayed connected to for almost forty years, and it never gets old; I never tire of it, and it never changes.

I think the lake is God.

I am SO grateful to have this space to come to rest, to rejuvenate, to heal, and to connect to my essence.

As I have said before, this place here is a perfect representation of my inner essence. That is why, whenever I arrive, I feel as though I have come home.

After my divorce in 2010, I was drawn to the beach as a place to soothe my broken heart and restore my soul from the many years of feeling lost and stuck in codependency. This was a local, convenient, and year-round accessible place for me to go on short breaks when my son was with his dad. I would pack up my lunch, an umbrella, and a chair and head to New Smyrna Beach, where the tides go out for hundreds of yards and the soft white sand extends for miles.

It is not crowded where I would go, so sometimes I would be the only chair around, except for the occasional walkers along the shore. I would walk, journal, do yoga, and allow the breeze to wash over my face. Sometimes, I would sit on the edge of where the water washed up on the shore, let the ripples flow over me, and dig deeper into the sand with each recession back out to sea. The sand exfoliated my skin, and the sea breeze exfoliated my mind. I felt at one with the ocean here. I felt God's presence around me. It felt easy to access the present moment and tune into whatever feelings and thoughts were raging inside me at the time. I would get clarity about something I might be worried about or begin to slow down enough to give myself permission to simply be.

I also felt pulled to let go of everything, if only for those few hours, and give in to the rhythm of the ocean waves. Many times, I would allow myself to lie entirely in the sand and water and release all my cares about what others might think of me as I surrendered to the mess of being sandy, of looking like a fool, and of anything else that my perfectionistic mind may have conjured up to limit me. I felt completely free and connected to the entire Universe.

The beach seemed to naturally connect me with an inner child who had been lying dormant for decades in my attempts to be so grown up from such an early age. I was playing house, wife, and adult right into my first marriage until it no longer felt like play. It was more like Halloween, and I couldn't wait to take my mask off. So, playing at the beach became a way to rediscover and reconnect with the little girl who needed to play for real. This was easy to do when my son and I would head to the beach together. He was six then, a boy who loved to run and sit in tide pools and was curious about crabs, fish, shells, and digging in the sand.

One day, we came to the beach with dear family friends. My friend was mom to my son's best friend. Our two boys were learning to boogie board in the waves. I felt called to teach them and found myself boogie boarding for the first time since I was a teenager. That day, laughing and riding the waves and listening to the squeals and excitement of these two precious boys whom I dearly loved (and still do!), my heart broke open, and I was able to connect with a feeling of love and freedom I had been disconnected from for a long time. It was as if the depression I had been drowning in had finally lifted. We hadn't a care in the world in those moments. We were all completely present. This is what it feels like to connect with your Source energy. Everything merges, and nothing is separate. Something as simple as an ocean, boogie boards, and the innocence of children provide you instant access.

○

During the weekends at the retreat center in Washington, which I have referred to throughout many of my stories, we would meet in a group room with a gigantic picture window looking out into the lush forest filled with gorgeous trees. We chanted in the mornings, facing this window, which also had a large altar in front of it adorned with candles, pictures, and other spiritual symbols. One morning, I opened my eyes while chanting a song titled "Ra Ma Da Sa," set to a waltz melody. The trees were flowing with the wind as if to the rhythm of the music. I felt particularly plugged in that morning and as if I was dancing with the trees. It was like God had reached out and swept me up, and we were all swaying together.

How you find Spirit in nature is as unique for you as your relationship with the Divine. Allow yourself to put on a new set of lenses as you observe the scenery surrounding you. Notice the life vibrating out of everything. Know that it is here for you. When everything else around you seems chaotic and crazy, nature is ever-present and never leaves. Nature is God, and it is there whenever you think to look or seek out a space to sit, walk, or lie down. Or, if you are inside, take a look outside your window. What do you see? What do you feel when you are in nature, wherever you may find yourself? Allow yourself to absorb the energy. Let it restore you and guide you deeper into your Self.

Chapter 11

Living the Promises of Love, Joy, Peace, and Abundance

Spiritual connection is powerful. I may even venture to say it is your most important relationship to cultivate and nurture. Fostering a strong connection to Spirit within you means that you will always have everything you need right where you are at any moment. All you ever have to do is take a deep breath, maybe close your eyes, and tune in.

As this book has unfolded, I have come to recognize that the promises of love, joy, peace, and abundance that emerge through this deep connection are antidotes to suffering. The tools provide you with ways to cultivate the connection and thus reveal a path that leads you out of a state of suffering and into a state of unlimited possibilities. Knowing a deep unconditional connection with Spirit is the source of true *love*. This is the antidote to loneliness. When you can plug into your unlimited potential, you experience *joy*. This is the antidote to feeling stuck.

Reclaiming your truth and knowing solidly who you are brings *peace*. This is the antidote to anxiety, restlessness, and fear. When your life begins to take the shape of a vision that was once beyond your dreams, you embrace *abundance*. This is the antidote to limited thinking and the fear that you will never have enough.

Practicing and using the tools I have shared with you will support you in discovering, nurturing, and strengthening your own personal connection to the Universal Source Energy that surrounds you, is in you, and *is* you. When you have a spiritual connection, you have the power to transform your life, move forward, and accomplish things that may seem impossible from your current vantage point. Practicing any one of the tools I have shared can be transformational. Practicing all of them becomes a superpower.

Throughout this book, I have shared snippets of my personal story of transformation. I always had a foundational connection with Spirit and was called back to it through each chapter of my life. However, the deterioration of my first marriage, getting divorced, and rebuilding my life was the catalyst for me to access more tools, expand my relationship with Spirit into something more all-encompassing, and fully integrate my spiritual connection into every waking moment. The tools I have shared with you are what I found to be most helpful in that integration.

I love sunflowers; they are the symbol of my business, Sol Flower Wellness, and they adorn the cover of this book. They represent a living being that grows toward the light. It is how I see you, my beloved reader. You are a spiritual seeker. You inherently and instinctively grow toward the light. But sometimes, you may get blinded or lose sight of the path. These tools are offered to help keep your vision clear and give you direction and support.

I cultivated all these tools in the garden of my heart; they helped me heal and ultimately turn my life into something I had only dreamed of and eventually into a life beyond anything I could have ever imagined on my own. Building upon each tool, they compounded my spiritual connection and allowed it to be stronger and more easily accessible than ever. Talk about an amazing church. I had church available to me anytime I needed it! I used all these tools to transform my life and inherited the gifts of love, joy, peace, and abundance along the way.

Journaling, nature, meditation, music, prayer, and ritual led me out of the treacherous waters of codependency and toxic relationships into a conscious relationship with my true-life partner. I released patterns of self-betrayal and learned how to set boundaries and settle for nothing less than what I knew I deserved. I successfully raised a son who is flourishing and knows how to speak his truth and remain true to himself. I built a sustainable business that financially and spiritually supports me. I brought my life from overcomplicated and draining into a simple, restorative, fulfilling life filled with everything I need and nothing that I don't. *I have more than enough for all I need* became my simple mantra.

I continue to use yoga to stay tuned into my body and work on healing my relationship with a distorted body image. It has also taught me to be more flexible both inside and out and to accept myself right where I am at any given moment.

I now understand that my spiritual connection is my inner knowing, and I listen to and trust in it completely. I trust in the cooperative nature of the Universe, and I know with absolute certainty that I am never, ever alone, and I have infinite choices available to me. I know for sure that by the grace of God and the power of prayer, all things are possible. These tools serve as my pathways to connection and are the foundation of everything I am grateful for in my life and all that I need to face whatever challenges await me throughout the rest of my time here on Earth. God is my ever-present companion, only a breath away.

My hope for you is that you will not have to stay as long in your own suffering or endure painful life events like divorce to begin your journey, although it seems that pain and suffering often draw us to surrender to something bigger. Or activate a longing for that spiritual connection. So, however you have found your way to this moment, you now have all the tools available to begin carving a new direction. Pick one or two tools to begin with and build your own matrix of whatever works best for you. Choose the ones that you connect with and leave the rest. Or try some out now and return to others at a different time or stage in your life. They are evergreen in their usefulness, and some may sit at the forefront for you depending on what you are experiencing at any given moment. This is not meant to be rigid. Flow with what feels right and begin to see what unfolds for you. Begin to access your spiritual connection when you think of it, but eventually allow it to integrate into your daily life, not so much as a task on your list but more as a constant companion that you lean into with each breath.

Practice gratitude as you take notice of the miracles and expansion that begin to occur in your life and even in those whose lives you touch. You emanate more light, feel lighter and freer, and your heart begins to open. You operate at a higher vibration that others start to notice and wonder how you emanate so much joy. You gradually connect deeper in relationships and see more clearly which relationships you want to bring closer and which ones may require more distance. You come to understand what true love feels like. You learn to feel more safe and secure knowing that you have a fully working inner compass that guides you toward your highest good and resonates with peace. Your new vibrational frequency, which originates from a most powerful Source, emits clear signals to attract all that you want and more. The possibilities are endless!

Chapter 12

Go Forth and Cultivate!

W hen you first picked up this book, you were looking for something. You wanted to cultivate a spiritual connection or strengthen an already existing one. You may have been seeking a way out of your own suffering or a pathway within, away from all the worldly distractions that constantly bombard you.

You now have the tools to create the experience you were seeking. But this will not happen if you finish this chapter and put this book on your bookshelf. The life and connection that you want to cultivate require action. If you are struggling to find the motivation or the energy or want someone else to make this happen for you, just close your eyes and take a breath. Send up a simple prayer and listen for the response. Or, take a walk outside without headphones, listen to the sounds, and breathe in the air. Feel the sun on your face and observe. Take one minute to breathe, raise your arms over your head, and stretch. One small thing at a time eventually builds into several small things that gradually evolve into a new direction, a new outlook, and, before you know it, a whole new life.

Take it slow. Enjoy the journey, and remember that there isn't actually a destination, only forward movement. You won't arrive anywhere, but you will be able to navigate any situation you find yourself in and always have a true north to return to. Love, joy, peace, and abundance will be more easily accessible, but those are not end points. They are ways to experience this life that you have been given to live here for a while on Earth. You are a spiritual being having a human experience. You now possess tools that will help you stay connected to that understanding and make for a much more fulfilling existence.

Now it's your turn!

What will you create? How will your life transform and/or be supported by these tools? What will your practice look like? What kind of relationship do you want to have with Spirit? What might you add to this toolbox? Follow your heart and use these tools to make something beautiful. You have all that you need within you. Take time to weed out what no longer serves you and cultivate the connection you deserve. Embrace a life of peace, a life full of joy, and a life overflowing with love and infinite abundance! You are worthy, you are strong, you are precious, and you are resourceful. I hold a vision of your heart expanding around all that flows toward you. Go forth and cultivate!

Recommended Reading

These are books and authors who have inspired my spiritual journey and helped me form the foundation of how I choose to live my life today. May you find inspiration in their words as you continue to explore and expand your worldview and life philosophy.

Beattie, Melody. *Codependent No More: How to Stop Controlling Others and Start Caring for Yourself.* Minnesota: Taylor & Francis, 1992.

Bernstein, Gabrielle. *The Universe Has Your Back: Transform Fear to Faith.* Hay House, Inc, 2016.

Cameron, Julia. *The Right to Write: An Invitation and Initiation into the Writing Life.* New York: TarcherPerigee, 1999.

Carrera, Jaganath. *Inside the Yoga Sutras: A Comprehensive Sourcebook for the Study and Practice of Patanjali's Yoga Sutras.* Buckingham, Va.: Integral Yoga Publications, 2005.

Cloud, Henry, and John Townsend. *Boundaries: When to Say Yes, How to Say No.* Zondervan, 2008.

Coelho, Paulo. *The Alchemist.* New York: SparkNotes, 2014.

Dalai Lama [Tenzin Gyatso] and Desmond Tutu. 2016. *The Book of Joy: Lasting Happiness in a Changing World.* With Douglas Abrams. New York: Avery.

Gibran, Kahlil. *The Prophet.* 1923. Reprint, New York: Alfred A. Knopf, 2018.

Gilbert, Elizabeth. *Big Magic: Creative Living Beyond Fear*. Riverhead Books, 2016.

————. *Eat, Pray, Love: One Woman's Search for Everything*. Bloomsbury Publishing PLC, 2010.

Girish. *Music and Mantras: The Yoga of Mindful Singing for Health, Happiness, Peace & Prosperity*. Simon and Schuster, 2016.

Gottman, John M. and Silver, Nan. *The Seven Principles for Making Marriage Work: A Practical Guide from the Country's Foremost Relationship Expert*. New York: Harmony Books, 2015.

Hendricks, Gay, and Hendricks, Kathlyn. *Conscious Loving: The Journey to Co-Commitment*. Bantam, 2009.

————. *The Conscious Heart: Seven Soul Choices That Create Your Relationship Destiny*. Bantam, 1999.

Hicks, Esther, and Hicks, Jerry. *Ask and It Is Given: Learning to Manifest Your Desires (Easyread Large Edition)*. ReadHowYouWant, 2009.

Lamott, Anne. *Help, Thanks, Wow: The Three Essential Prayers*. New York: Riverhead Books, 2012.

Rohr, Richard. *Breathing under Water: Spirituality and the Twelve Steps*. Newburyport: Franciscan Media, 2021.

Ruiz, Don, Miguel. *The Four Agreements: A Practical Guide to Personal Freedom*. San Rafael, Ca: Amber-Allen, 1997.

Schnarch, David. *Passionate Marriage: Keeping Love & Intimacy Alive in Committed Relationships*, W. W. Norton & Company,1997.

Schucman, Helen, and Thetford, Bill. *A Course in Miracles.* Createspace Independent Publishing Platform, 2016.

Singer, Michael A. *The Untethered Soul: The Journey Beyond Yourself.* ReadHowYouWant. 2009.

Taylor, Jill Bolte. *My Stroke of Insight: A Brain Scientist's Personal Journey.* New York: Viking, 2008.

Tolle, Eckhart. *The Power of Now: A Guide to Spiritual Enlightenment.* Sydney, NSW: Hodder Headline PLC, 2000.

Tolle, Eckhart. *A New Earth: Awakening to Your Life's Purpose.* Penguin. Audio, (narrated by author), 2005.

Walker, Alice. *The Color Purple.* New York: Harcourt Brace & Jovanovich, 1982.

Young, William, P., Jacobsen, Wayne and Cummings, Brad. *The Shack.* Los Angeles: Windblown Media, 2007.

Recommended Playlist for Chanting, Meditation, and Inspiration

Have fun with this! Mix and match, explore the artists further, and find what resonates with your heart and soul. Happy listening!

Songs for Chanting:

Ajeet. *Ra Ma Da Sa Healing.*

Ashana. *Opening to Love.*

Ashana. *Ave Maria.*

Beekman, Johanna. *Hallelujah Govinda.*

———. *Heart Beats One.*

———. *Om Shanti (Peace in Our Hearts).*

Das, Ananda. *Om Namo Bhagavate.*

Das, Krishna. *All One (Hare Krishna).*

———. *By Your Grace/ Jai Gurudev.*

———. *Goddess Prayer.*

———. *Ma Durga.*

———. *Mountain Hare Krishna.*

———. *Om Namah Shivaya.*

———. *Om Namoh Bhagavate Vasudevaya.*

De Lory, Donna. *Hey Ma Durga (Donna De Lory/Mac Quayle Mix).*

Girish. *Diamonds in the Sun.*

———. *Ganapati.*

———. *Jaya Ganesh.*

———. *Kali Durge.*

———. *Lakshmi.*

———. *Ra Ma Da Sa.*

———. *Saraswati.*

Jai-Jagdeesh. *I Am Thine.*

———. *Mayray Govindaa.*

———. *Ong Namo Guru Dayvaa.*

———. *With You.*

———. *Om Namah Shivaya Raam.*

Kaur, Sirgun. *Amen.*

Kaur, Snatam. *Aad Guray Nameh.*

———. *By Thy Grace.*

———. *Ek Ong Kar Sat Nam.*

———. *Long Time Sun.*

———. *Ra Ma Da Sa.*

———, *Anand (Bliss).*

———. *Ong Namo.*

Premal, Deva. *Gayatri Mantra.*

———. *Om Namo Bhagavate.*

Rob and Melissa. *Gayatri Mantra.*

———. *Guru Invocation.*

———. *Jai Sri Ram.*

———. *Lakshmi.*

———. *Maha Mrityunjaya.*

———. *Prayer for Peace.*

———. *Radhe Govinda.*

———. *Tejase.*

Singh, Sat Darshan, and Kaur, Sirgun. *Bliss (I Am the Light of My Soul).*

Stringer, Dave. *Ganapati Om.*

———. *Kali Durge.*

———. *Om Namo Bhagavate.*

Wertheimer, Benjy and Heather. *Shantala: Om Namo Bhagavate/Because the One I Love.*

White, C. C. *Karuna Sagari Ma.*

Songs for Meditation:

Anugama. *Chakra Journey.*

———. *Healing Earth (Earth Frequency Meditation).*

———. *Mystical Trance.*

———. *Shamanic Dream.*

Fjallgren, Jon Henrik. *Daniel's Joik.*

———. *My First Love.*

Raye, Marina. *Awakened Heart.*

———. *Gentle Nature.*

———. *Invitation.*

———. *Radiance.*

Van Sickle, Kurt. *Make Me an Instrument.*

———. *Mother Divine.*

———. *River of Life.*

Songs for Inspiration:

Bliss. *A Hundred Thousand Angels.*

Brickman, Jim. *Never Alone.*

The Canadian Tenors. *Hallelujah.*

Denver, John. *Calypso.*

———. *Gospel Changes.*

———. *Let It Be.*

———. *Poems, Prayers, and Promises.*

———. *Rocky Mountain High.*

———. *Sweet Surrender.*

———. *Windsong.*

———. *Looking for Space.*

Drucker, Karen. *If Love Is Why I'm Here.*

———. *Let Go of the Shore.*

———. *Morning Prayer: I Will Surrender.*

Elevation Worship. *Graves into Gardens.*

The Fray. *Be Still.*

Gokey, Danny. *New Day.* Radio Version.

Groban, Josh. *You Raise Me Up.*

Kaleo. *How I Love You.*

Kaur, Dev Suroop. *On This Day/Long Time Sun.*

Laird, Lydia. *Hallelujah Even Here.*

Matisyahu. *Live like a Warrior.*

———. *Miracle.*

———. *Sunshine.*

Mraz, Jason. *Everything Is Sound.*

———. *God Rests in Reason.*

———. *Life Is Wonderful.*

———. *Living in the Moment.*

Premal, Deva & Mitten. *There Is so Much Magnificence.*

Stapleton, Chris. *Broken Halos.*

Third Day, *Call My Name.*

———. *Cry out to Jesus.*

———. *I Will Always Be True.*

———. *Mountain of God.*

———. *Revelation.*

Williams, Zach. *Fear Is a Liar.*

———, *Freedom.*

Williams, Zach, and Parton, Dolly. *There Was Jesus.*

Zac Brown Band. *Let It Go.*

———. *Quiet Your Mind.*

———. *Remedy.*

———. *Tomorrow Never Comes.*

Acknowledgments

I felt called to write a book back in college. I have spent the last thirty years sitting in ambivalence, procrastination, wishing, hoping, dreaming, starting, stopping, and spinning in circles. I began to wonder if I would ever write a book and fulfill this dream that seemed to originate from deep within my soul. I just did not know yet *how* to make it a reality. Then, I met Dr. Richard Nongard at a hypnosis conference in March 2023 and signed up for his class, "Write a Book with Richard." This class is designed to help you write a book within twelve weeks. For some reason, when this opportunity presented itself, I knew that this was my how. Thank you, Richard, for giving me the tools, encouraging me to write through my fears and perfectionism, and helping me see that this was possible. I now have this book to share, along with many more books yet to be birthed, that now have a pathway into the world. Words cannot express the value of this meeting. Thank you to Tamelynda Lux for being willing to work with a new author and to help make this manuscript ready for publication.

Without my mastermind group, which meets every week religiously, I would not have had a space to keep this dream at the forefront even as it got put off year after year after year. . . until this year. Shahn, Sarah, and Kurt: your love, support, and belief in me and my writing helped to carry me when I doubted myself and kept me clear and present throughout this whole journey.

To my beloved family and dearest friends, I am eternally grateful for your support of my writing through the years, for reading my blogs and newsletters, for encouraging me as a writer, and for holding the belief that one day I would write a book. To my precious son, Breck, for inspiring me to be better every day. And to my husband, David, for being the one I can be myself with while be-ing together.

And finally, to you, my dear reader. Thank you for being willing to pick up this book and supporting my dream to share words on a page. To help this work reach more readers, please consider leaving a review wherever you shop for books. Thank you does not even begin to express my gratitude and appreciation.

About the Author

Wendy E. Crane is a licensed marriage and family therapist in Central Florida and the owner of Sol Flower Wellness. Wendy provides individual, couples, and family therapy, hypnotherapy, and online coaching programs. She combines her clinical training with certifications as a hypnotherapist and Kripalu yoga teacher to offer an approach to mental health and well-being that integrates mind, body, and spirit. Her style is conversational and compassionate. She seeks to connect with you on a deep level and challenges you to break out of old limiting beliefs and behaviors. She is passionate about empowering you to grow and expand to your greatest potential. She lives near Orlando with her forever husband in their quaint little College Park cottage and is filling her empty nest with writing and learning new ways to expand her creativity. You can learn more about Wendy and her offerings at www.solflowerwellness.com.

If you would like to contact Wendy for more information about her services or to schedule her for a speaking engagement with your company or organization, you may reach her by email at wendy@solflowerwellness.com. To stay informed about future books, programs, and other resources Wendy offers, please join her mailing list from her website. When you share your email, you will receive a free e-book full of resources to help you *Jumpstart Your Journey.*